A
TENURED
PROFESSOR

A NOVEL

John Kenneth Galbraith

A MARINER BOOK

Houghton Mifflin Company

BOSTON   NEW YORK

FIRST MARINER BOOKS EDITION 2001

Visit our Web site: www.houghtonmifflinbooks.com.

Library of Congress Cataloging-in-Publication Data
Galbraith, John Kenneth, date.
A tenured professor / John Kenneth Galbraith.
p.   cm.
ISBN 0-618-15455-8
I. Title.
PS3557.A4113T46   1990
813'.54—dc20   89-39559 CIP

Book design by Anne Chalmers

Printed in the United States of America

QUM 10 9 8 7 6 5 4 3 2 1

A
TENURED
PROFESSOR

Books by John Kenneth Galbraith

American Capitalism: The Concept of Countervailing Power

A Theory of Price Control

The Great Crash, 1929

The Affluent Society

The McLandress Dimension

The Scotch

The New Industrial State

The Triumph

Indian Painting (with Mohinder Singh Randhawa)

Ambassador's Journal

Economics and Public Purpose

Money: Whence It Came, Where It Went

Annals of an Abiding Liberal

A Life in Our Times

The Anatomy of Power

A View from the Stands

Economics in Perspective: A Critical History

A Tenured Professor

The Culture of Contentment

A Journey Through Economic Time: A Firsthand View

The Good Society: The Humane Agenda

Name-Dropping: From F.D.R. On

The Essential Galbraith

"Why didn't someone tell me about banking before?"

With one exception, none of the persons here celebrated teaches at Harvard or otherwise exists. To
Professor McCrimmon I have assigned certain academic tendencies and attitudes which, over the
years, I have sought to resist in myself.

The Harvard Faculty Club, recently "gentrified,"
is described as of the time of this history.

As this book goes to press, the President and the
Congress of the United States are contemplating
reform as regards Political Action Committees, the
PACs. Whatever the outcome, the solution here offered is preferred.

A
TENURED
PROFESSOR

· 1 ·

THE LONG

TABLE

HARVARD YARD, the ancient center of college and university instruction, is an enclosure of a bit more than twenty acres in extent that is now the site only of libraries, a few classrooms, the handsome administration building, a number of dormitories for the entering class, a church and the stretch of greensward on which the annual commencement ceremonies are held. Students in medicine, public health, dentistry, business administration, and some in the sciences and the law see it rarely, if at all. However, for all Harvard men and women it is thought a place of great symbolic, nostalgic and liturgical importance; there is something slightly solemn in a reference to *the Yard*. Once, when speaking there, John F. Kennedy told of his pleasure in being back on the Harvard *campus*. The reaction was severe. It is recognized that busy politicians do not always write their own speeches. But it was considered far from fitting that this should be so starkly confirmed by a Harvard man, along with the obvious fact that he hadn't read over beforehand what he was going to say.

On one side of the Yard is Quincy Street, a one-way thoroughfare that separates it from the art museum, a center for the study of the visual arts and a dining hall for the freshmen. When women were first admitted to Harvard residence, the designation of "freshperson" was briefly attempted, but it didn't succeed.

Also across Quincy Street from a well-traversed gate out of the Yard is the Faculty Club. This is a structure of unconvincingly Georgian aspect; like many Harvard buildings it conveys the impression that both architect and architecture were something of an afterthought. Inside the club on the ground floor are a spacious entry hall and, to the left, beyond a small reception desk and some cloakrooms, a large, rectangular, well-lighted room in which, it was once hoped, faculty members would gather to read and converse after lunch, making it perhaps a center of social concourse for the university. This has not happened.

The room and the furniture are unattractive and give the impression of having been shabby even when new. There are newspapers available, but, by late noon, they have become disassembled and dog-eared, the only exceptions being *The Times* of London and some other overseas journals, added to accord a cosmopolitan touch, which no one is ever seen to read. There are also magazines, many of which, by the inadvertence of magazine subscription, continue to come free. At some point a coffee urn and cups were placed on one of the tables to encourage after-lunch relaxation and talk. These too have not been a success.

Such social purpose as is served by the club is accomplished in the three dining rooms spread away to the right of the entry hall. Here for two or three hours at midday there is an agreeable sense of activity. Waitresses and an occasional waiter move about, providing food with surprising efficiency. The decor, if undistinguished, is not unpleasant. Few pause to regard the large oil portraits that look down from the walls, gifts long ago to the university museums that were not considered good enough for more reputable display. No one so pictured is now known.

At one end of the largest of the dining rooms and close by the doorways leading on to the other two is the long table. This, by common consent, is the major communications center of the university. A professor of classics once suggested it be called the college *epicentrum,* another effort that didn't take.

At the smaller tables in the three rooms younger scholars gather for purposeful discussion or to entertain the numerous visitors to the university who, faithful to an established academic tradition that makes movement a substitute for thought, travel to Cambridge in pursuit of some scientific or literary enterprise which, too often, has only a ritualistic aspect. Older professors, quite a few retired members of the faculty and those with no particular luncheon companion for the day go to the long table. All hope that in the course of the meal they will pick up some interesting or even useful information; in this they are frequently disappointed. The daily exchange runs generally to personal history and anecdotes, these being at Harvard, as elsewhere, a major teaching resource. In past times when Harvard professors returned from service in

Washington — with the State Department, the Pentagon, the OSS or less reputably with the CIA or the Labor Department — the recapture of their public achievements in face of extreme bureaucratic or legislative error often served as primary lecture material for a term. Students were thought to be impressed.

Sometimes, however, the conversation at the long table takes a more useful turn — to some crisis in the management of university affairs; some portent of disaster in international relations on which a scholar with presumed knowledge will be questioned in a reflective way; some aberration by a statesman, like Ronald Reagan, of whom grave disapproval is assumed; or to the current preoccupation of the faculty or the Faculty Council, where for some time legislation on sexual harassment has been an urgent topic. Referred to by the Faculty Council as "amorous relationships in the instructional context," this was, at first, the problem, admittedly exceptional, of unduly ardent professors, assistant professors and teaching assistants who offered better grades or threatened worse ones as an inducement to what was called sexual preferment. Later, however, attention shifted to some notably enterprising young women who, it was alleged, threatened their teachers with a charge of such sexual aggression unless they were given the marks they felt they deserved.

Very often a professor comes to the long table with some topic in mind and engages others in his concerns with little regard for their interest or attention.

· · ·

So it happened on the day when this history begins. Two professors of middle years — one tall, with sparse red hair, thin, elongated features, deep-set eyes and a gen-

5

erally distinguished bearing; the other shorter, slightly fleshed around the jowls and with, in contrast to his companion, an air of extreme good nature — arrived briskly at the long table just after one o'clock. It is a time when the early diners, including retired professors who are brought promptly to their meal by reluctantly admitted idleness, are beginning to leave. The newcomers nodded briefly to their neighbors; the latter nodded back.

"How are you, Ted?" The question was to the tall, red-haired man.

"You are looking well, Professor Grierson," said another. It was evident that Grierson was a man of standing, a presence of some prestige at the long table. He, after a brief response, continued with the conversation he was having with his companion on the way to the club.

"It could," he said, "be a major breakthrough."

"I agree, if it holds up. A quantum step."

"I'm not too sure of all the details, but it's a new concept and he seems to be giving it a pretty solid trial."

"Why doesn't he go ahead and publish?"

"He wants to keep it to himself for a while. It's his way of doing things. Also his wife's. She has a strong voice in these matters. Pretty active in politics as well."

"Well, politics and personal life *are* one's own business. Or should be."

"Yes, they should be," said Grierson. "It's his economics that counts, in any case. That's what we got him back here from Berkeley for. We really got something, I think."

. . .

"What have your economists come up with now, Grierson?"

The interruption came from a solidly built man wearing a heavy green Harris tweed jacket with a sweater and bow tie. His clean-shaven face was round and pink; his nearly white hair was brushed with obvious attention on two sides of the well-marked, also very pink, line of the part. At first glance he seemed a man of genial aspect; only on a closer look did one see that his eyes, small, alert and unblinking, were unequivocally mean. The question could, perhaps, have been expected.

Angus Maxwell McCrimmon, professor of advanced psychometrics, now in his late fifties, would, in earlier times, have been approaching retirement. He was in his accustomed place near the end of the long table, his back to the clutter and conversation of the dining room. Neither there nor elsewhere was McCrimmon a figure of affection. Recalling the noted Scottish saying on the Clan McCrimmon, a professor of Celtic once observed that at Harvard things were different: "Where the McCrimmon sits is the *foot* of the table." Angus McCrimmon's character was not one that emerged gradually as he became known. In this history he is, as he was at Harvard, an evident earth-fault in an otherwise stable terrain.

In every university a decent harmony is maintained only as a steady flow of minor faculty misjudgments, misadventures and misdemeanors is overlooked, ignored, forgiven. Mild descents into plagiarism, an otherwise too obvious misappropriation of the ideas of others, a too transparent tendency to intellectual mystification, an unduly evident surrender to dubious outside sponsorship of research, a book depicted by the scholar as of unparalleled power and interest that, regrettably, remains always one year in the future, are all accepted as inevitable. They are passed over except in the most intimate conversation and ignored to the extent possible by the university administration. The alternative is acrimony and recrimination, and these are hostile to the community spirit that allows men and women of varying character and achievement to live peacefully together.

To McCrimmon, however, tolerance and discretion were unknown. By nothing had he felt so rewarded over the years as by the aberrations of his colleagues and the mistakes and miscalculations of presidents, deans and governing boards. When a consensus had been reached at a faculty meeting, it was McCrimmon who spoke ardently to its flaws. When he found himself in the majority, he went eloquently into the opposition.

Only with students was McCrimmon exempt from the hostility he was known greatly to enjoy. That was because, with the exception of some flagrant eccentrics, he had no students. Partly this derived from general undergraduate ignorance, shared by much of the faculty, as to what psychometrics was. McCrimmon, however, had a different view.

"Years ago Kirsopp Lake made his reputation at Harvard by giving its easiest course and thereby equipping thousands of students with a wholly unnecessary knowledge of the Bible. I give the hardest course, and thus I maintain standards, don't spoil the undergraduates with easily acquired information and leave myself with time for more important personal matters."

Not for many years had the *Confi-Guide,* a student publication which annually reports on the diligence and competence of Harvard professors and the content of their courses, had a paragraph on McCrimmon. No one ever came forward with a judgment, for few with a minimal sense of purpose had ever finished a term in his course.

McCrimmon, having gotten Grierson's attention, continued: "A breakthrough, you say? If it's in economics, at least it can't be dangerous. Nothing like gene engineering, laser beams, sex hormones or international relations. That's where we don't want any breakthroughs."

"Nothing dangerous, Mac," said Professor Grierson with a slight edge to his voice, "but very interesting for us. A good predictive model by our Professor Marvin. You should know about him — one of our bright young people. Even you might be impressed."

He came down firmly on the words "even you." As usual, it didn't work.

"You'll have to explain. I've seen references to economic models in the papers before. What's new about this one?"

Professor Grierson looked at his luncheon companion, who was appreciatively eating a Reuben sandwich. This was now a lunchtime staple at the long table in succession to horse steak, a favorite in the difficult days during and after World War II and for many years a tradition on the menu. His fellow economist didn't respond. Grierson drew a slight breath.

"A good model replicates the American or world economy or some part of it, gives you a working view of its operation, tells you what it will do in the future."

"You mean recessions, depressions, unemployment, inflation and the other misfortunes you arrange for us? Profits in various industries? What will happen to the stock market?"

Professor Grierson decided to shorten his answers.

"A good model has predictive value. That about sums it up."

This, too, didn't work. By now others at the long table were suspending their conversation to listen. Only at the extreme end was there still talk on a mooted change in undergraduate course requirements — a liberalization in the required or core curriculum that was thought by the more sensitive teachers to pose grave educational risks. As McCrimmon had long ago discovered, the truly offensive aspects of his personality were a reliable source of attention.

"Don't you already have these models? What about the one in Lexington, also invented, as I remember, by a Harvard professor? Data Resources or some such. That excellent man Eckstein. Doesn't that work?"

"Yes, of course it does," said Grierson. "And there are Wharton Econometrics and others."

"Aren't they reliable? Why do we need another?"

"They do sometimes miss the boat. That's how economic prediction is; it sometimes gets blown off course."

"Your maritime metaphors impress me. If predictions aren't reliable, of what value are they?"

Grierson was near the end of his patience. People generally accepted his word, and he had come to expect it. But he knew that one didn't show anger or even impatience at the long table; it couldn't be thought that McCrimmon had gotten one's goat.

"To put it simply, the American businessman, in his business planning, has to have something better than a guess."

"So a wrong prediction is better than a guess?"

"A prediction is something to go on," said Grierson.

"It narrows the range of uncertainty for the business firm. And for the government too."

"You're saying that uncertainty is reduced by a wrong prediction but increased by a wrong guess?"

Rescue was at hand. Professor Grierson's colleague, having just lighted a small cigar, shook out the match and moved in to help.

"These matters," he said with some finality, "can be understood only in the administrative context of the modern business enterprise. Any guess as to the future — about sales, production costs, profits — is the ultimate responsibility of the executive making it. That for him is a major personal risk; it means he must put his career on the line. A prediction derived from a predictive model, on the other hand, comes from a highly responsible outside source. Accordingly, it greatly reduces the area of personal uncertainty and danger for anyone who must deal with the future. I really think, sir, that's pretty obvious."

McCrimmon seemed appeased. "That makes sense to me. That's what this model will do? Remove any error to another party?"

Grierson came back into the conversation, his voice now harder than before. There was lost ground to retrieve. "By no means. The Marvin model is affirmatively predictive in a new sense."

"Sorry, I misunderstood. You must explain."

"Other models, other perceptions of the future, assume rational behavior, rational responses, rational expectations. Marvin, on the other hand, identifies, isolates, measures and acts on irrational expectations. He has discovered that people who are making money or who hope to make money mentally adjust the world to their hopes. He operates on other people's error."

McCrimmon's response was now almost mellow, something that all regarded as menacing. "I can understand how irrational expectations are a great improvement over rational ones. But how does your man Marvin identify these expectations?"

"That, to some extent, is Marvin's secret. He is keeping his confidence at least until he's pretty sure of his system. Reasonably sure."

"Does his system work on the stock market?"

"Definitely."

"Then why doesn't he test it out with his own money?"

Matters had at last turned in Grierson's favor. "That," he said, "is precisely what he is doing."

"Is he rich?"

"No, he's been with us only a few years."

"Some of us have been here longer than that without getting into the Milken bracket. Or even Henry Kissinger's."

. . .

It was clear in spite of his aggressive tone that McCrimmon was impressed. That a young professor might be using his own resources to test his personal theories of human behavior was unprecedented in academic life. McCrimmon smiled in what he intended to be a genial way and subsided. His enjoyment of his own unpleasantness had always been in the process and not the result. After some especially talented exercise in nastiness, he and his victim frequently parted on quite civil terms. Professor Grierson returned to his coffee; a professor from across the table leaned forward to ask "Do you really think he might make money out of this — if it works?"

Although the question was addressed to Grierson, a well-tailored, clean-shaven man on his right took it up.

"There's nothing wrong with that. Over at the Business School we give money a lot of attention. We don't see it as evil. Not at all."

"Dr. Johnson said, 'There are few ways in which a man can be more innocently employed than in getting money.' " Another professor had intervened.

"He also said, 'It matters not how a man dies, but how he lives.' "

"Yeah, and he said, 'I am willing to love all mankind except an American.' "

"To me, I must say, Samuel Johnson is something of a bore."

"That's certainly not the view of Jackson Bate."

The long table was back to normal.

. . .

"I hear you have a problem down at your house, Grierson." Harvard upperclassmen and -women have houses, not just dormitories; an important and agreeable distinction.

"It's something we didn't foresee. Neither the master nor any of us. It's going to happen in the other houses too."

"What's it all about?"

The conversation was not only back to normal but back to sex.

"Well, we've taken a particularly strong stand against harassment. Tutors pressing themselves on female students. And vice versa. That kind of behavior. Now we have a case where a couple, a teaching assistant and a student, have fallen genuinely in love."

"You never thought of that?" Again it was Mc-Crimmon.

"Of course we didn't. Naturally it never occurred to anyone. But we think we have a solution."

"What's that?"

"In all such cases they will register with the master. Then it will be legitimate and aboveboard."

"But not above bed," said McCrimmon. "What you'll have then will be licensed as distinct from unlicensed sex. I suppose it's a useful distinction."

Professor Grierson chose not to reply. He looked at his watch, he and his colleague scraped their chairs back, and, checking again with the clock over the door, they passed on to the cloakroom and out into the sunshine.

.   .   .

A few minutes later they were followed by McCrimmon. Walking across the Yard in front of Widener Library and then along beside Massachusetts Hall, the oldest of Harvard buildings, which now houses the offices of the president, he made his way through the traffic in the upper part of Harvard Square. Glancing around out of habit to see that he was unnoticed, he went into the recently refurbished movie theatre. Once one great hall for the display and breathless admiration of Pickford, Chaplin, Swanson, Grant, Cooper and Bacall, it was now divided into five anonymous cubicles, each with its equally anonymous offering. Professor McCrimmon chose one at random and settled down for the afternoon.

· 2 ·

DISCLOSURE

JOE CRAFTWIN, the managing editor, looked out from his small, square, desolate office at the fringe of the city room of *The Boston Globe,* the leading and, in the view of the avowedly better residents of the metropolis, the only newspaper in Boston and its environs. A short, compact man, professionally indifferent in tailoring, he had a voice that despite many years of effort had acquired only a moderately convincing tone of authority. At the desks, which stretched into the near distance, men and an occasional woman eyed their computer screens as they typed, deleted and corrected. Others leaned back in their chairs in poorly simulated thought. Over all was an aspect of quiet, continuous movement, literary effort now conformed to industrial process.

From the door Craftwin signaled to one of the more ostentatiously idle of the room's inhabitants, who moved gradually down the aisle. A large man, seriously overweight, with what is known in Boston as a pleasant Irish face, he entered the small room and stood towering over the editor. Craftwin pulled from his pocket a book of notes and leafed through the pages.

"I got word from one of the Harvards of a new wrinkle in economics. Economic forecasting. Probably nothing to it, there never is, but if there is, *The Wall Street Journal* will be all over the place. Get out there and see what you can learn. It's more for you than the financials, I think. The guy's name is Marvin."

"Any idea where I find him?"

"Yeah. I heard last night at the Vice-President's speech at the Kennedy School. He's moving today into one of those big houses on Brattle Street. They don't see how he can afford it. This might be your chance. They say he doesn't like being interviewed, so you might catch him unloading his word processor."

"What's the true gen?" It had long been a matter for comment around the city room that Eldon Carroll was an avid student of Hemingway and rejoiced especially in his more flagrant military lingo. He had once proposed himself to Craftwin for a posting to Beirut; it would be like Madrid during the Spanish Civil War. Craftwin had demurred; modern conflict, especially that in the Middle East, lacked the Spanish distinction. Carroll remained on the Boston educational beat: Harvard, MIT, Tufts, Boston University, Boston College, occasionally out to distant Wellesley College. In all these great institutions people scanned the paper for mention of colleagues newly honored or published or suddenly in descent into serious marital or academic disgrace.

Craftwin continued: "Something having to do with expectations — irrational expectations or some such. It assumes that everyone in business is a little insane. He must have had some newspaper experience. That's about all I know. You can take a car. Oh, and Ellen says there's a woman's angle. His wife is very strong with the liberationists; keeps him on a short leash, they say."

. . .

Brattle Street stretches west from Harvard Square for a little more than a mile. There is no thoroughfare like it anywhere in the United States. The houses, most of them built in the eighteenth and nineteenth centuries, owe their interest almost entirely to their size. Each was designed on a grander scale than the one before. But trees and shrubbery conceal the worst architectural features, and some, most notably the house that sheltered Henry Wadsworth Longfellow in its greatest days, arouse the interest, even excitement, of the elderly occupants of the sightseeing buses that daily ply the street.

Years ago these vast dwellings were home to the literary and social elite of the United States, including, besides Longfellow, numerous professors at Harvard. Small blue signs by the front doors or on the gateposts still celebrate past occupants of great distinction, many of them now unfamiliar to the modern tourist.

Not for some time, however, have Harvard professors dependent on their salary been able to afford these mansions. Nor are their wives still available for the large and complex tasks imposed by the necessary upkeep. Most women must work, and, a more subtle point, they no longer seek, in the manner of competitors at a country fair, pre-eminence in the social and culinary arts. Therefore the present occupants of these vast structures, eccentric exceptions apart, are not commonly known in the academic community. Presumably they are adequately affluent, but at Harvard that has never been an acceptable route to acclaim.

.   .   .

It was into one of these houses, nonetheless, that the young Montgomery Marvin, economics professor, was moving. Eldon Carroll, having found a parking place nearby, walked past a large van in the driveway and identified Professor Marvin without difficulty as the person supervising the passage of a battered mahogany desk through the side door off the spacious verandah that encircled most of the house. Although it was a lovely spring day and the trees, flowering shrubs and narcissi that grace the street were in full bloom, there was still a breath of cool air coming across the porch. Marvin, lean of face with a sharply trimmed beard, was in slacks, checked shirt and a Windbreaker. He would have been in nowise noticeable in a crowd. When the desk was inside, he acknowledged Eldon Carroll's presence without enthusiasm.

"I'm from the *Globe,* and I thought I might have a word with you." Eldon was aware that, as an opening gambit, this lacked originality.

"You probably see that I'm pretty busy." Saying this, Marvin looked at not one but three personal computers sitting side by side on the porch next to a large stack of printout paper, two desk chairs and several metal filing cabinets.

"I can see that. Will this house be your office?"

"Oh, no," said Marvin. "I have my office at the university. Littauer Center. But I like to do a certain amount of my work at home, and some of my assistants can come out here occasionally to help me." He waved his hand at the house. "My wife and my children and I hardly need this much space."

"Could you tell me a little about this new forecasting system you have developed? We've been hearing about it at the paper. We want to be sure that whatever we say about it is correct."

Professor Marvin recognized the ploy. His reply was disconcerting. "I wouldn't worry too much about that. Misinformation, even disinformation, is fairly common in economic reporting. You're allowed an occasional lapse. Things would be pretty hard for you otherwise."

Eldon Carroll ignored the distraction. "This looks like a fairly expensive house. Do you play the market yourself?"

He thought this a long and slightly dangerous shot, but it didn't work. Professor Marvin's face clouded over ever so slightly. "I wouldn't want to comment on that. A personal matter, you know." He turned to pick up a large wastepaper basket.

Carroll saw it was useless to press the point. He smiled and changed the subject. "Could you tell me a little about your background, Professor?"

Marvin relaxed. "Sure. I was born in New York. Westchester County, to be exact. Harvard, Cambridge University. Doctorate at Berkeley before coming here. That's it. I wonder, though, if you would excuse me. You can see how much I still have to do."

Waving a hand, he turned and walked into the house.

Carroll faced the fact: it would take more imagination than he could readily mobilize to make anything out of this story. He returned to his car, circled the block back beyond Harvard Square and turned in beside the huge William James Hall, home of sociologists, psychologists, psychometricists and a few anthropologists. He parked in a space reserved for a scholar named Cairncross and, checking the directory, rode the elevator to the floor on which he would find Professor Angus Maxwell McCrimmon.

Anyone in the newspaper business distinguishes between those who really know and those who are known to be available. Reporters seeking information around Harvard had long come to regard McCrimmon as available.

Today he was in his office, a light and airy room, the walls lined with bookcases filled rather ostentatiously with technical journals. A small desk was relatively uncluttered; a large filing cabinet bore the label WORK IN PROGRESS. McCrimmon had evidently been resting on a sofa upholstered in a rather boisterous pattern of red and brown. He greeted his visitor and then stretched himself out again on the couch, his arms under his head.

"Of course I know about this Marvin business. I make a point of keeping myself informed on what goes on here. There's nothing to it. Grierson, whom you probably know, gave me the details. Economists make these forecasts and sell them to business corporations, where they become the basis for decisions. Coming from outside, they get the executive off the hook when he has to decide how many cars to make or whether to put a new product on the market, say some innovative pornography. There *is* money in forecasting, but I hear that it's getting to be a pretty competitive business."

"That's very helpful, Professor," said Carroll. "Anything else I should know?"

McCrimmon sensed that he had given away too much too soon. A change of pace was in order; he must be more reticent. "There might, in fact, be something to it in this case. This lad Marvin seems to be testing the system himself before selling it. And I'm told that from his profits he's just bought a big house on Beacon Hill, over in Boston. But there's another, larger aspect."

"What's that?"

"Marvin has come up with a new idea. It might be the subject of my next book. We talk and teach about how to do things right — how to follow the correct course. We ought to be concerned with all the forces that make people do what is crazy. That, I gather, is Marvin's view. We suffer far more from human error than we gain from our occasional lapse into good sense. Follow me?"

Carroll had stopped taking notes. "Perfectly, Professor. How do you feel about Professor Marvin testing out his system with his own money? Maybe doing a little speculating on his own account?"

"As I said, that's greatly to his credit. But he'll probably get involved in insider trading. That could be a problem for the dean."

Carroll folded up his notebook. "Thanks ever so much, Professor. You've made everything very clear."

McCrimmon half rose to shake hands. "Give my best," he said in a friendly, seemingly knowledgeable way, "to your Mr. Murdoch."

Carroll departed, and McCrimmon subsided gratefully

onto the couch. It was thus that he regularly received his occasional visitor, the even more occasional student. Emerson once said that nothing so impairs intellectual achievement as exposure to physical activity, and McCrimmon believed in carrying that advice to the plausible limit. He couldn't help the feeling that in the interview he had done well.

. . .

Back at the newspaper in the big building located inconveniently out of town on the road to the unduly remote Kennedy Library, the equally remote University of Massachusetts and on down to Cape Cod, Eldon Carroll did the best he could with the story. There was something there. The computers, the other office equipment, the house, Professor Montgomery Marvin's confidence-inspiring reticence. A lesser man would have done at least a little self-promotion. There was also that restrained response to the question about playing the stock market. But only a little of this could be put up on the computer screen; it is the fate of the journalist always to know more than he can safely print.

Later that day Joe Craftwin looked at the copy and called Carroll in. "There might be something here. But you forgot about the woman's angle. His wife. Also my friend Grierson. See what he knows."

Grierson was in his house in the nearby suburb of Belmont and answered the phone himself. After confirming that Marvin did have a new "predictive system," he indicated that it might be a breakthrough.

Carroll asked him about the role of Professor Marvin's wife.

"I wouldn't wish to comment on the family affairs of one of my colleagues," replied Grierson. He was rather firm.

Carroll acknowledged the question of comradely good taste involved but asked if there was anything at all Professor Grierson could say about Mrs. Marvin.

"She's a very able woman. A good wife and mother, I'm sure. Definitely on the liberal side and very strongminded. Aggressive, perhaps you could say. I think she drives Professor Marvin fairly hard. She and her friends. They are very strong on women's rights, which, I may add, I favor."

"Does she help him on this forecasting?"

"No, but she gets him involved with her social causes. So far, though, it hasn't interfered too much with his scholarly work. He was a student of mine a few years back."

"I hear they might be making a bucket of money."

"As I say, I wouldn't want to comment in any way on any personal matters."

.   .   ' .

"It might be a good story," said Craftwin to the makeup man, "but we'd probably better play it safe. Put it back with the truss ads."

And so it appeared. "ECONOMIC FORECASTING. Harvard Professor's New Design. Irrational Economic Behavior Assumed. Wife in Commanding Role." The substance of the article was disappointing, but it was read with interest in Cambridge and not wholly ignored elsewhere.

· 3 ·

THE CULTURE OF
SUBVERSION, I

"I'M DELIGHTED by your decision to become an economist. You will, I'm sure, be a very distinguished scholar in our field." The words were addressed to Montgomery Marvin; they came from his tutor, the still quite young Professor Grierson. The two men were in the comfortable if somewhat shopworn living room of his suite in Dunster House, one of the twelve residential houses that accommodate upperclassmen and -women at Harvard. These contain living quarters, dining rooms, libraries, common rooms and in one case a swimming pool and are also, in a modest way, centers of instruction. Pleasantly red-brick Georgian in aspect like most of the others, Dunster House celebrates the memory of Henry Dunster, the first fully designated president of Harvard; one Nathaniel Eaton having served from 1637 to 1639 but never having been given the title. According to legend, the intention had been to name the original seven houses for Harvard presidents in their order of succession, a design that faltered when it came to the notable Dr. Leonard Hoar, who came to this distinguished post in 1672, a mere thirty-six years after the founding of the university. Hoar House had an indelicacy of address that, even in the service of history, Harvard could not abide. It was decided to honor instead two modern presidents, Charles William Eliot and Abbott Lawrence Lowell.

"I like economics," said Marvin, "especially the technical side. But perhaps I can also do some good in the world."

"Excellent," said Professor Grierson, "but watch that business about doing good. It's fine in principle, but a smart economist sticks to his knitting. So stick to it. Don't get diverted by a lot of political and public activities. That sort of thing has taken a good many economists down the tubes. Some in other fields too. Look at Kissinger. It's more than enough to be a good scholar."

"Didn't Adam Smith have political influence? Pitt thought so, said he was a guide to all public policy. And what about Keynes?" Sessions with one's tutor at Harvard favor an argumentative technique.

"Smith's influence came entirely from his *Wealth of Nations;* his job as customs collector was a late-in-life sinecure. And Keynes's influence came from his *General Theory* and his book on the economic consequences of Versailles. He didn't get involved in politics until very much later. Bretton Woods. Your influence should be through your writing."

"Didn't Keynes make money in the stock market?"

"Quite a bit, by the standards of the time. I see no objection to that."

"Surely that got him away from his scholarly work?"

"Not seriously. Purely private activities. And he used the money to support his college and the arts. Why don't we have one more session next week?"

Montgomery Marvin's Harvard education was coming to an end. He stopped briefly by his rooms and then made his way out to walk a somewhat circuitous route along the Charles River toward a final lecture in the Yard. Professor Grierson returned to his reading; he was glad that once more he had helped someone see the importance of sticking to his knitting.

.   .   .

There was much in his tutor's injunction that Montgomery Marvin welcomed; he liked a quiet life. The relevancies and irrelevancies of economics he had found enjoyable, and this enjoyment was sustained by his competent and relatively easy mastery of the subject. But still lurking somewhere in his subconscious was the feeling that he wanted something more. In truth, Marvin could not entirely escape his family background, one that assumed, even if it did not emphasize, a certain political commitment. And while he was not old enough to be truly influenced by the 1960s, he was certainly a child of the still troubled 1970s.

Montgomery Marvin had been born in the agreeably suburban town of Mamaroneck, New York, from which his father commuted each day to Manhattan to serve in the advertising firm of Marvin, Montgomery and Manion, known to the relatively few who had heard of it as the Three Ms. In later years, as he became a man of fame and ill fame, Montgomery Marvin would see his antecedents traced by imaginative journalists to the great St.

Paul corporation Minnesota Mining and Manufacturing, which bears the stock market designation MMM. This was both wrong and out of scale. The Madison Avenue MMM was neither large nor remunerative — it prided itself on taking neither tobacco nor alcohol advertising, none having ever been offered, and in being available to such public interest enterprises as those of Ralph Nader, Common Cause and People for the American Way. It had arranged television spots for the political campaigns of such socially responsive liberals as Adlai Stevenson, Hubert Humphrey and John Lindsay when he was mayor of New York, but none of these contributed greatly to revenues.

It was, in fact, on a few old and tolerant accounts, notably those of the more recondite pharmaceutical and medical suppliers, that the firm survived. From these to Joseph Marvin came enough money to send his only son to Exeter and on to Harvard. And from Joseph Marvin to Montgomery Marvin came the sense that one should be involved in socially significant activities. The elder Marvin had served conscientiously on local town committees, the library board and once as a delegate to a Democratic convention in Chicago in support of Adlai Stevenson.

At Exeter Montgomery Marvin, always known in later years as Marvin — Montgomery didn't lend itself to everyday use, and Monty didn't suit such a serious and self-contained young man — was diligent, successful and, in a general way, unhappy. As a liberal reflecting his father's modestly avowed faith, he had an adverse sense of the political indifference of his fellow students. He also reacted to the appalling gloom of the dormitory to which he was assigned. And to the clinical depression of his roommate, a sallow youth from Tupelo, Mississippi, who had been sent north to gain competitive stature in the declining world of the WASPs and who was bitterly homesick.

Only in Marvin's last year did his life improve; his roommate, now withdrawn from the school following a largely demonstrative attempt at suicide, had been replaced by an emotionally stable, exceptionally bright and diligent Chinese student, an aspiring entrepreneur, one of the first wave of an eventual flood from Taiwan. He questioned Marvin at length on his political orientation and commitment and made clear his regret that his own intended preoccupation with business would exclude such concerns. On graduation, Marvin, whose grades were more than adequate, passed easily into Harvard, where in all respects his life was better.

.   .   .

He arrived in Cambridge in the autumn of 1972, the year of the McGovern debacle. There was still at the university a resonance from the worldwide revolt of the 1960s — of Danny the Red in Paris, Mark Rudd at Columbia University and Mario Savio at Berkeley, the 1969 seizure by the Harvard students of University Hall and the violent resort to the State Police by the mentally somewhat vulnerable university president of the day. Marvin was not unaffected. These events were the conditioning factors of his generation and thus of his own life.

There was also the continuing specter of the Vietnam war, which now had a strongly personal aspect. The automatic college deferments were gone; no longer were undergraduates or graduate students a privileged and protected group. Remaining only was the near certainty that, if drafted, they would serve in operations well removed from the rice paddies and the jungle. This was not new. It was known in World War II that no soldier with an advanced academic or professional degree, unless irrationally motivated, ever heard a shot fired in anger.

Marvin's solution, however, was, in the main, to stick to his studies, and in these he both did well and found a measure of relief and protection from his conscience. There was also protection in the words of Professor Grierson, and he felt it that morning as he walked along the river.

He even received some measure of reassurance from the local scene. He passed the graceful Weeks Bridge, worthy of the Seine and honoring a family prominent in Massachusetts and national life and politics who, over several generations, had made no departure from the economic and social principles avowed by Herbert Spencer and Herbert Hoover (and later, if more casually, by Ronald Reagan). These were the survival of the fittest and the belief in wealth as a source of prestige and power, that wealth being the benign endowment of a discriminating Creator. Such views had enjoyed no slight measure of acclaim and were here commemorated. Were they not a lesson for his generation?

Also, looking across the river, he saw the buildings of the Harvard School of Business Administration. These, in an impressively more opulent Georgian style than those on the Cambridge side of the Charles, gave a further sense of reassurance. Money, it was there said and devoutly believed, was the scorecard of life. With so many so convinced, perhaps he could be exempt from personal unease.

Perhaps, as with Keynes, money could be made that would support some higher purpose. He walked by the intended site of the Kennedy School of Government. Better, he thought, the pursuit of academic distinction than the barren symbols and rituals of Washington.

Harvard students are known, not least to themselves, for the depth and range of their perception. Marvin could not escape the feeling that morning that few had ever brought it to bear so sharply on themselves.

.   .   .

During his Harvard years Marvin had concentrated on economics, statistics, social psychology, and once, attracted by the title of the course, he had made a highly eccentric detour into psychometrics. Thereafter he was more respectful of the advice of his fellow students, who from common knowledge had advised him against it. Professor McCrimmon had inveighed powerfully to the handful present against sobriety, rationality and good sense as social assumptions. Better to assume individual and collective aberration. Or, at a minimum, the truth of the controlling concepts of Freud and Jung as they led to aberrant behavior. In a more than slightly mystifying exercise, he outlined his method for assessing and measuring the absurdities of individuals and groups. Around Thanksgiving the course came to an end; McCrimmon handed out a reading list and announced that he had nothing more to say.

There were more rewarding experiences. Marvin took a course under Professor Wassily Leontief, then in his final year at Harvard, winner of the Nobel Prize for Economics and the most innovative of American economists. It was Leontief who had first made a statistical model of the American economy, a massive construct showing what each industry received in income from every other, what each supplied in purchases to all the others, how the whole structure moved together. It was a design that was to remain firmly in Marvin's mind. If one could predict the overall movement, one could know how each individual industry would fare. Were the McCrimmon elements of euphoria and pessimism put into the prediction, they would be reflected down to individual industries and firms. Arbitrage would be possible as between irrationality and reality. If one invested in opposition to irrationality, money — again that forbidding word — could be made when reality asserted itself. It was all a vague gleam, an evanescent sparkle, in Marvin's stream of thought. But it was already there.

.   .   .

Marvin's activities had not been wholly academic; he had shown an interest in undergraduate theatre and intercollegiate sports that he did not altogether feel. He was conscious of the need for what Thorstein Veblen called the "good repute" of his community. He had also exercised conscientiously in the indoor athletic building, where he swam the required number of lengths each afternoon. In much the same spirit, he had had an undemanding liaison with an intelligent woman who lived in the next entry but one to his own. An admiring follower of Gloria Steinem, an aspiring writer and a rapt student in comparative literature of the noted Professor Levin, she too had, as it was coming to be called, her own agenda. In pursuit of that, sex had only a passive and therapeutic function.

Under the guidance of Professor Grierson, Marvin

wrote a senior thesis on psychological and psychiatric impulse in economic behavior as manifested in the Leontief model. Though not fully understood, it was well received. He graduated *summa cum laude* and was offered a Marshall Scholarship, honoring George C. Marshall and the Marshall Plan, at the University of Cambridge. Having no other academic opportunity at hand, he immediately accepted. He listened to Art Buchwald and Daniel Patrick Moynihan at the Class Day and commencement exercises and departed to spend the summer in Vienna. He had heard from his friends of the special grandeur of that capital; he would there improve his German and in those highly appropriate surroundings deepen his appreciation of Freud and Jung.

.   .   .

Not far from the Vienna Opera and St. Stephen's Cathedral is the Karlskirche, a handsomely elaborate Baroque church facing a pleasant garden with benches, a pond where children sail boats and feed the ducks, and admirably tended flower beds filled with startling red flowers. This was only a few blocks from where Marvin had found inexpensive lodgings; he went there to read whenever the weather was bright and warm, as often that summer it was. He felt, although he did not like to admit it, more than a little lonely.

One morning, however, his reading was interrupted when a young woman, slightly taller than he, not slender but not quite robust in appearance and clad in a workmanlike skirt and jacket of blue, unfaded denim, sat down on the bench beside him and said, "You're Montgomery Marvin, aren't you?"

He asked how she knew.

"I was told by a friend who goes to Harvard that I might find you here. I couldn't have picked you out of a crowd, but I saw what you were reading."

Marvin held up Joseph Schumpeter's *Capitalism, Socialism, and Democracy*, in which he had taken refuge from Freud's letters.

"Very reactionary," she said.

"Not altogether. He's kind to Marx, says here that he was 'a very learned man.' That's not bad."

"Yes, but the book is a hymn of praise for capitalism, even though he thinks the system won't survive. But it's too nice a morning to argue. You're going on to Cambridge, aren't you?"

Marvin said he was and asked as to her plans.

"My name is Marjorie Bradford. I'm called Marjie. I'm a Canadian, University of Toronto. I went there hoping to study under Robertson Davies, but then I got trapped into economics. I'm here on my way to Oxford. I have a Balogh Fellowship at Balliol. You know about Lord Balogh?"

"Only vaguely. Aren't you troubled being under the auspices of a lord?"

"Not Lord *Balogh*," she said. "You should be ashamed of yourself. The most disliked man in Britain. Never can resist the truth. One of two great Hungarians — Nicholas Kaldor and Thomas Balogh. They are called Buddha and Pest. Both have made it to the House of Lords. Greatly to Britain's credit."

Marvin and Marjie continued to talk and then went together to lunch. The next day they met again and went out to Schoenbrunn. On their return after dinner, they went to Marvin's room. His Austrian landlady viewed his companion in a tolerant way and stopped him next morning to tell him the room would be more money for two.

His friend at Dunster House had viewed sex as a clinical exercise. Marjie, in contrast, was exuberant. So, rather to his surprise, was he.

Preparing for bed a night or two later, he said, "I wish you were coming to Cambridge."

She said, "Oh, I'll be coming over. There are people there I particularly want to see. Joan Robinson. Kaldor too. His daughter Mary. Do you know about the NDP?"

"I've heard of it, of course. The Canadian New Democratic Party."

"You're better informed than most Americans. I'm going home to work for it, make it over. I want a party that offends and frightens all the best people in the United States. To be respected, we Canadians must learn to seem a trifle dangerous."

"That's very logical," said Marvin. "But why not come to the United States and be dangerous there?"

"Why not?" said Marjie. "But now we must go to sleep."

In ensuing days they went to the opera, out again to Schoenbrunn, and once, getting visas with impressive ease, they took the boat down the Danube to Budapest. A late-middle-aged professor at the university to whom Marjie had an introduction took them to dinner and told them that socialism and communism were functionally unimportant.

"Look at Eastern Europe. The Czechs, Hungarians, Slovaks, Slovenes and some of the Poles do well. That's because their territories were all in the old Empire. The Rumanians, Serbs, Bulgarians, Montenegrins and the rest of the Poles do badly. That's because they were outside. The important thing is not the social system but the history. That must trace to a culturally advanced monarchy. Those who are the captives of ideology deserve only our pity or contempt. We should do everything we can to make their lives miserable."

The lecture continued until it was time for them to go back to their lodgings. The professor saw them away with a final word. "Remember, I have it from one of your own scribes: 'If you can't comfort the afflicted, you can at least afflict the comfortable.' It's what I try to do here."

Marvin and Marjie took the train back to Vienna and a few days later the plane to Heathrow. They separated at the airport, Marjie going directly to Oxford and Marvin taking the bus into London and the train on to Cambridge.

It was now the autumn of 1976, and Jimmy Carter was soon to be President of the United States. A well-meaning, honest, attractive and seriously insecure man, he would be the hapless victim of his orthodox, presumptively liberal and relentlessly damaging economists and of his even more disastrous foreign policy advisers, with their unshakable commitment to the high respectability associated with the Cold War. Of none of this was Montgomery Marvin aware when he arrived in Cambridge. Nor were very many of his fellow citizens at home.

He did know that he was going to study in the place where Alfred Marshall had brought classical economics to its highest, perhaps even its final, state of perfection.

And where had been born the economic design to be identified durably with the name John Maynard Keynes. Cambridge was also the scene of the subversion of Kim Philby, Guy Burgess, Donald Maclean and Anthony Blount. Although no one in the university suspected it — nor, certainly, did Montgomery Marvin — a new subversive design was in the making. For this too the ancient courts of learning would have a measure of responsibility.

· 4 ·

THE CULTURE OF

SUBVERSION, II

DECENTLY ATTIRED in a grey suit and trench coat, now growing a trim beard in response to a plea from Marjie but otherwise wholly commonplace in appearance, Marvin, with two large suitcases, arrived at the Porter's Lodge inside Trinity Great Gate, Cambridge, on a September day in 1976. Someone had told him that, as an aspiring economist, he should apply to King's, a few steps down Trinity Street and King's Parade. That college celebrated a past association with Keynes, the estimable A. C. Pigou, who was known for having brought the word "welfare" into economic use, and a younger generation of economic scholars, now no longer young, of radical and reformist instinct. Of these Marvin had heard; he intended to seek them out. But he was also told that, as a Marshall Scholar, he had a wide selection as to college, and it would be considered eccentric to make Trinity a second choice. No one, it was said, ever had.

The porter greeted him affably, and his assistant guided

Marvin across Trinity Great Court to his rooms in Nevile's Court and showed him the location of the not closely
adjacent toilet and bath.

Looking out from his window across the perfectly
manicured grass on which only Fellows of the College
were allowed to walk, and to the superb and serene Wren
Library enclosing the end of the court, Marvin thought
that never before had his surroundings seemed so perfect,
and he asked himself the inevitable question: Why not
put aside the larger, more obtrusive, more demanding
and more perilous claims of life and settle for this or some
similar academic calm? His mind then turned to Marjie
and to his own inner compulsions, and he knew that it
was impossible. There still remained, however, the matter of defining the path and the goal.

In the ensuing months, far more explicitly than he
could have hoped, both path and goal began to appear.

.   .   .

The path emerged with some slight clarity one mild and
lovely late December evening — winter in England, as
compared with that in New England, is a nominal thing.
Marvin was returning from a barely comprehensible lecture by a professor from the University of Virginia —
the first of that year's Marshall Lectures, which are given
annually to preserve the memory of Alfred Marshall.
Peering through the light gloom, he saw a vaguely familiar figure crossing the Great Court. As they grew
nearer to each other, it proved to be Professor Mc-
Crimmon. Marvin identified himself with some hesita-
tion as a former Harvard student; McCrimmon expressed
pleasure and invited him to stop by the Old Guest Room,

where he was quartered. He had been attending a conference on new developments in Social Psychometric Theory and Method at the University of Manchester. Having become bored, he had left soon after it opened to come and visit an old friend at Trinity, but his friend had discovered after McCrimmon's arrival that he had an urgent engagement for the evening. To that sort of thing Professor McCrimmon was somewhat accustomed; he seemed glad to have company.

He and Marvin settled into chairs of extreme discomfort, in keeping with the general aspect of the room, and McCrimmon asked Marvin what he was doing at Cambridge and what were his plans for his life.

"I'm going to be an economist, but I want to make my small contribution to the liberal agenda. Peace, a better break for the poor and the inner cities, greater equality in income distribution, government assuming its proper responsibilities. I haven't got it fully worked out yet."

"Most unwise," said McCrimmon, adding with some emphasis, "most unwise. And certainly impractical."

"Why, sir?"

"You simply won't get tenure. Tenure was originally invented to protect radical professors, those who challenged the accepted order. But we don't have such people anymore at the universities, and the reason *is* tenure. When the time comes to grant it nowadays, the radicals get screened out. That's its principal function. It's a very good system, really — keeps academic life at a decent level of tranquillity."

"Suppose one waits until one has tenure to show one's liberal tendencies?" Marvin felt obliged to make some response.

"The only sensible course," said McCrimmon. "But

by then conformity will be a habit. You'll no longer be a threat to the peace and comfort of our ivied walls. The system really works."

There seemed no point in pursuing the subject. Marvin asked about the meetings McCrimmon had been attending.

"A ritual," said McCrimmon, "in which, as a professor, I feel required to participate. You listen for an hour to a paper you could have read in fifteen minutes. Or, in practice, not read at all. But tell me, what do you do with your time here?"

"I go to lectures."

"Are they any good?"

"I have one professor who reads the proofs of his next book. Sometimes a page slips away onto the floor before he gets to it, and he doesn't even notice. I was told that the same thing happened with Keynes."

"Lectures," said McCrimmon, "are our most flexible art form. Any idea, however slight, can be expanded to fill fifty-five minutes; any idea, however great, can be condensed to that time. And if no ideas are available, there can always be discussion. Discussion is the vacuum that fills a vacuum. If no one comes to your lectures or seminars, you can have a workshop and get your colleagues involved. They have to come, and your reputation as an adequately popular teacher is saved."

By this time McCrimmon had kicked off his shoes. Now he got up and removed his tie. It was clear that the meeting was over. He repeated once more, "Remember what I told you about tenure."

Marvin made his way back to his own rooms.

· · ·

A further step in Marvin's guidance came in these days from his reading. This was pleasantly undirected, and it took him more or less by chance to the great financial episodes of earlier and modern times. One day in Heffer's, the lovely bookstore down the street from Trinity Great Gate, he came across a book on the history of Bernard Cornfeld and Investors Overseas Services, and from it he learned, not without admiration, what one individual had accomplished in the uninhibited world of high finance. Operating near Geneva, in the shadow of the great house in which Voltaire had lived, Cornfeld had extracted many, many millions of dollars from eager investors. No special genius was involved; it was surely what anyone could do. His operations ended in disaster, but was there not a more secure design? Foreseeing disaster, might not one make money before it eventually struck?

From Cornfeld and Geneva Marvin went back a full three centuries to the Tulipomania in Holland, the wild and wonderful speculation in the price of tulip bulbs in which a single bulb was sometimes worth more than the farm on which it was grown. Then, in 1637, the resounding collapse. He read about John Law, the peripatetic and financially innovative Scot whose Compagnie d'Occident aroused the interest of all Paris for its pursuit of the great gold deposits of Louisiana, gold that to this day has been found only by individual malefactors in the treasury of that state. And once more the collapse — this time in July of 1720, in one of the most spectacular of all rushes to get out.

In England there was the immortal South Sea Company of these same years, featuring among other undertakings one "of great advantage, but nobody to know what it is." The euphoria surrounding the company's works, which were heavily blessed by the government, resulted in the price of its stock rising irresistibly from £130 in early 1720 to £1020 by the middle of that year, the upsurge being followed in August by the inevitable crash. This was known at the time and became famous in the annals of financial history as the South Sea Bubble.

Marvin went on in his reading to the slightly more mundane follies of the nineteenth century in the United States — the turnpike- and canal-building boom of the 1820s and 1830s, and the railroad boom, which reached its peak in the 1880s. Again the eagerness of investors, many of them British, to be parted from their money, as soon, after spectacular defaults, they were. Along the way he encountered one of the less pedestrian but more wholly successful promotions of its time, a company organized in England to drain the Red Sea in order to retrieve the treasure dropped by the Egyptians when the Israelites passed through the divided waters. Eventually he came down to the great Wall Street boom of 1927, 1928 and 1929. Once again the eagerness of the moneyed classes to divest themselves of their resources. Some wealth being had, all caution was sacrificed in the hope for more.

Marvin reflected at odd moments on the meaning of his odyssey. Great tragedy, certainly, but with nothing being lost but money. The astonishing capacity of capitalism to punish most those who, for a time, it had most lavishly rewarded. But, above all, the extreme predictability of these episodes. In one form or another they recurred — reliably. First the willing surrender of money, then the drastic expropriation. Inherent in the economic system was the tendency of people who were presumptively sane to be captured by euphoria, to be guided not by reality but by what served their own superbly conditioned hopes. One day he happened on an observation by Walter Bagehot, the long-time editor of *The Economist* and the most literate and perceptive of economic journalists. "People," Bagehot said, "are most credulous when they are most happy . . ."

The lectures Marvin had attended at Harvard, the McCrimmon effusions apart, and those he now heard at this historic locus of economic thought assumed rationality. This was the economist's compliment to his own world — the business and financial world. Clearly, on frequent occasion, one could assume the opposite.

And might there not be financial advantage from doing so? Marvin's reading, from the tulip disaster down to the Great Crash of 1929, had told uniformly, even relentlessly, of the losses that had been incurred. This, surely, was right as regards those who had bought. But what of those who had sold? They didn't lose; they emerged in wonderful but anonymous wealth. Somewhere, somehow, with each loss there was also some gain.

With a slight sense of guilt in those months — he felt he should be doing something of greater economic import — Marvin read the memoirs of the Duc de Saint-Simon. Reflecting on the collapse of Law's Mississippi Scheme and the Banque Royale, whose notes had financed that debacle and more pertinently the debts of the French government and of Philippe, Duc d'Orléans, the regent, Saint-Simon commented on the "tiny minority" who had been "enriched by the total ruin of all the rest of the people." The thought echoed in Marvin's mind: let one assume insanity and be of that tiny minority.

.   .   .

On weekends that year Marvin traveled regularly up to London and on to Oxford. There he joined Marjie, first in exceptionally dismal lodgings — a bed-sitter — across St. Giles' from Balliol and then, rather to his surprise, in a pleasant two-room suite in the Randolph Hotel.

"It seems, " she said, "that I can afford it." She went on to explain. A great-aunt of Tory stock, the designation in Canada being United Empire Loyalist, had gone from Ontario as a young woman to be the bride of a businessman in Maine, the scion of an old Bangor firm given to the manufacture of bone wear and buttons. The business had long since disappeared; it had too righteously resisted the step on to plastics. The old lady had outlived all plausible heirs, and after a variety of local bequests, she had left the residue of her estate to Marjie, who had visited her from Toronto during several summers.

"The lawyer doesn't yet know how much I get," said Marjie, "maybe quite something. Some General Electric stock purchased directly from Thomas Edison; IBM that came personally from your Thomas Watson, Senior. Great capital gains. He told me I could safely live better, and I detested that other place. I'm for the poor, but I'm not for personal squalor."

.   .   .

In February Marjie drove over to visit Marvin in Cambridge and remained for several days; she had acquired a Volkswagen. Not far from Queens' College, set squarely on the Cam by the locks that regulate its exceptionally modest flow, is the Garden House Hotel; this too was now within her means. Later she came again. Marvin journeyed back and forth to the hotel from Trinity; it was pleasant, he discovered, to have ready access to a bathroom and, even more, to a toilet.

Marvin's circle of acquaintances had by this time widened in the college and in the university. Marjie, informed and forthcoming in all academic discussion, intelligently firm in her views and vigorous in manner and appearance, was more than a good companion; she added impressively to his standing with both teachers and student contemporaries.

.   .   .

One afternoon during her second visit they went through Trinity, across the river and along the Backs at the invitation of a married couple, both professors of economics, both of mature years. The four of them sat in the square, half-dark living room over tea, which was soon followed by sherry. The face of neither husband nor wife was fully visible; the voice of the latter, nonetheless, came through both loud and clear. She seized with evident pleasure on the opportunity to instruct two young North Americans, members of an unquestionably influential but, regrettably, more than slightly retarded race.

The conversation began on economic development — the errors of American policy in the poor countries, as she called them, scrupulously avoiding the emerging reference to a Third World. "All Americans assume that what is right for the United States is right for Ghana or Kampala. If it's done in Pittsburgh, that's all you think you need to know. Steel mills, shiny airports, dams. Above all, airports and dams. You don't read your own history. If you did, you would know that the really important things — schools, normal schools, roads, stable

government — come first. And that the only people who
are reliably efficient, productive and totally happy in their
economic life are the independent farmers. There you
have the rewards of exploitation. Bless them, they exploit
themselves *and* their wives *and* their children."

Marvin tried to signal approval on a subject to which
he had given no thought. Even Marjie was silent. However, through the gloom she too seemed to be nodding
her head in agreement.

The professor now shifted to a new subject, the political
ineffectiveness of American liberals, on which her husband added a word of assent from time to time.

"You're one of those liberals, I'm sure," she said, addressing Marvin so far as anyone could tell, "and when
you go home, you'll be like all the rest. You'll complain
constantly about the power of money and do nothing
about it. Complaining but compliant. That's all."

"What *should* I do?" asked Marvin.

"It's obvious. Get money yourself and then exercise
power yourself. Don't waste your time asking others to
be nice; do right."

"That might not be so easy," said Marvin.

"Just look at the people who get rich. No particular
intelligence. Americans especially. Anyhow, if you don't
know how to get money, you have no business calling
yourself an economist. If untrained, stupid people can get
rich, why can't you? Be like Maynard; he died a wealthy
man by the standards of the time. And he didn't work
at it more than an hour a day. Why try to persuade politicians when you can buy them?"

"I don't think we can all be quite up to Keynes in this
matter," said Marvin, but Marjie broke in. "I think it's

a neat idea. If wealth is the instrument of power, then get hold of that instrument. I'd be all for that, Marvin."

The conversation continued. Their hostess re-emphasized the point. "At least be rich enough so that you can do all the socially inconvenient things without personal risk. That's the true formula for happiness."

Later Marvin and Marjie made their way back across the river to the hotel. At dinner that evening Marjie left Marvin in no doubt: she had been impressed.

"It's the perfectly obvious course. I'd like to be in on it." There was then an echo of an earlier conversation in Vienna: "Perhaps it *would* be more fun in the United States than in Canada."

"Is that a proposal?" asked Marvin.

"As you prefer," said Marjie.

.   .   .

Some time earlier that winter Marvin had been led to wonder if he should do all of his graduate work at Cambridge, and, in doubt, he had sent in applications to Berkeley, Yale and, after some thought, the University of Chicago. Nothing would so confer respectability, a conservative aura, as to study in the economic tradition of the most relentless of conservatives, the noted Professor Milton Friedman. Lurking in his mind was McCrimmon's formula for success and tenure. He had acceptances from all and a telegram from the chairman of the economics department at Berkeley encouraging him to come.

He accepted California. The Berkeley reputation especially attracted Marjie. They decided that they would go to Italy for a couple of spring and early summer

months before visiting Marjie's ailing father in Toronto — her mother was long since dead. Then they
would go on to Marvin's parents in Mamaroneck. His
father, faced with early and unwelcome retirement, was
mildly depressed and contemplating a move to Sarasota.

In Amalfi, by an Italian priest who understood no En-
glish and assumed that anyone so motivated as to seek
him out was safely Catholic, Montgomery Marvin and
Marjorie Bradford were joined in an indubitably holy
wedlock.

· 5 ·

CALIFORNIA
INTERLUDE

THE BERKELEY CAMPUS of the University of California slopes down from the hills behind and looks out on the great bay below; the Golden Gate and its wonderfully graceful bridge are in the far distance. Mount Tamalpais is off to the west, with its recumbent mistress visible down its side. The campus buildings of the early twentieth century and before are in the pseudo-Moorish-revival tradition once rightly favored in California. Later structures reflect the stark misfortune of cost-benefit analysis but do not entirely dominate the scene. Berkeley remains the most aesthetically favored concourse for learning anywhere in the world.

Marvin and Marjie arrived on this seminal approach to paradise in the early autumn of 1977. Having come by air, they were pleasantly devoid of possessions. Spurning the more spacious and elegant accommodations to the north and above the campus, they found a decently comfortable furnished apartment, the upper half of a two-family dwelling, well on the road to proletarian Oakland.

Marjie's financial position had by this time clarified, the cautionary prose of the lawyers notwithstanding. She would, it appeared, be modestly affluent. Their living quarters, though undistinguished, reflected no ostentatious effort to simulate poverty. In keeping with what was now a fairly clearly perceived design, these would be the years of preparation, and the Marvins would be unobtrusive in the best tradition of high scholarship.

But not all was subject to plan. Montgomery Marvin was by nature an unobtrusive man. And Marjie, who was normally by no means unobtrusive, was for the time prepared to conform. She too enrolled in the established routine of graduate courses — macroeconomics, called by the inner learned "macro," and microeconomic theory, called "micro" for all conversational purposes. Her performance, if at times unduly forceful, was acceptable; Marvin's was brilliant. As the first year passed, word circulated through the department, through Barrows Hall, the center of economics instruction, that they were, indeed, a very good "husband-and-wife team."

"Do you really want to be a member of a team?" Marvin asked Marjie when they heard of this characterization of their scholarly standing.

"I don't mind at all," said Marjie. "I have every intention of dominating it. Or, anyhow, of keeping you from sitting comfortably on your ass."

"Couldn't you just relax and be happy in these surroundings?"

"Certainly, but when did we decide that this was life? This is preparation for life."

．　　．　　．

In the course of that preparation, Marvin now went beyond the field of economics as commonly perceived. At Harvard he had taken courses in moderately advanced mathematics; at Berkeley he ventured on into the more esoteric reaches of the subject, where he was confident he could find guidance and support for work on the more sophisticated levels of economic theory. There, by common consent, was where true academic achievement lay. He remembered another comment made by the distinguished woman professor he and Marjie had visited that evening in Cambridge.

"Never forget, dear boy, that academic distinction in economics is not to be had from giving a clear account of how the world works. Keynes knew that; had he made his *General Theory* completely comprehensible, it would have been ignored. Economists value most the colleague whom they most struggle to understand. The pride they feel in eventually succeeding leads to admiration for the man who set them so difficult a task. And anyone who cannot be understood at all will be especially admired. All will want to give the impression that they have penetrated his mystification. This accords him a standing above all others."

Talking with his fellow students, listening to his professors, reading the economic journals, Marvin concluded his British friend had indeed identified the plausible path to professional distinction. It was one he would follow.

Additionally, there was, he came to understand, the matter of specialization. It too was very important. No one, it was clear, was so suspect as the scholar who was said to "spread himself too thin." That he must never do.

. . .

In keeping with these conclusions, Marvin did a paper for his advanced course in microeconomic theory that year on "Mathematical Paradigms in an Approach to Refrigerator Pricing." The subject had come to him one night when their home freezer went on the blink. It was a remarkable piece of work, involving a fascinating display of competence in both differential and integral calculus as well as an impressive proliferation of algebraic equations. His professor, understanding it in the main, had it Xeroxed and circulated among his colleagues. Marvin was henceforth regarded with respect mixed with mild envy by his fellow graduate students and even by some of the younger faculty.

After a year and a few months at Berkeley, Marvin, with some course credits transferred in a highly informal fashion from Cambridge, took the preliminary examination for his Ph.D. Much of it centered on his refrigerator paper; he passed brilliantly and was invited to teach a section in the elementary course in economics. He declined, explaining that he wished to devote himself to research. He wanted, he said, to expand his early work on refrigerator prices into a full-scale doctor's thesis.

It was known by this time that the Marvins were not seriously in need of money. It is that need which supplies young scholars for instructional toil in all American universities at prices highly advantageous to their employers. Nonetheless, when, somewhat later, Marjie, who had also passed her first Ph.D. examination, was offered a job as an assistant in one of the large undergraduate courses, she promptly accepted. She told Marvin that she was determined to correct some of the more obvious misinformation offered in the lectures.

Two years had passed since their arrival in Berkeley.

The California seasons — wet and dry, green and brown, distinctive but never violent — had come and gone. Finally accepting their mild affluence, Marvin and Marjie moved into slightly more spacious living arrangements to the north of the campus, a pleasant apartment with a view over the bay and a special room that could accommodate their two computers, the printer, several filing cabinets, some books and a long and littered table. They still kept to themselves but not excessively so.

Berkeley, more than most academic communities, is a place of many social levels. At the top are the great university officials — president, chancellor, deans and the recognized professorial stars, those known for their Nobel Prizes, their urgently discussed books, their occasionally urgent summonses to Washington.

Next comes the large, undifferentiated band of scholars, teachers and scientists, not excluding those who, nervously aware of the frequent condemnation of their occupation, commute daily to the east of the hills to work at the Livermore Laboratories, which are operated for the government by the California university system. There they uneasily contemplate the possible destruction of the planet, their own possible role therein and the ill repute in which they fear they are held by the undergraduates and numerous of their neighbors.

Farther down the social scale are the students, the tradesmen and those who, after surveying the larger scene, have quite simply found Berkeley the most agreeable of places in which to live.

In this more than normally varied amalgam the Marvins continued to attract only slight attention. That they were liberal in motivation was taken for granted; in this community it was noticeable, if not eccentric, to be otherwise. They attended meetings for Ronald V. Dellums, the most reliably radical member of the House of Representatives, contributed modestly to his campaigns and made friends in nearby Oakland with Jessica Mitford, the local representative of the politically most diverse, brilliant and in important respects most disastrous of British families. Inevitably they supported sanctuary for refugees from El Salvador, applauded Rose Bird when she became chief justice of the California Supreme Court, opposed offshore oil concessions and deeply regretted the continuing political relevance of Ronald Reagan.

On one occasion they were invited with other younger economists to the home of a former president of the university, once a professor of economics himself and in no small measure the architect and builder of the great California university system, a breathtaking achievement. They heard him tell of his coming to this enormous task and of his departure after collision with Governor Reagan: "I left as I arrived, fired with enthusiasm." On the way home Marjie, as she usually did, summarized what they'd heard and its bearing on their own design. "He said it: most people are kept in line by the fear of loss. It's the great disciplinary force of the Establishment. But he wasn't. He lost big because he won big. That's my idea of life."

. . .

Approaching his subject carefully, Marvin wrote his Ph.D. thesis on the same topic and under the same title as his earlier and noted term paper. It was, all who read it agreed, a small marvel of technical and mathematical exegesis.

"You have advanced not only the interpretive theory

of refrigerator pricing but the whole science of mathematical and paradigmatic price analysis," an admiring
professor wrote in comment. Marvin's examination on
the thesis was an exercise in mildly competitive con-
gratulation; his committee was joined by the professor of
Applied Agricultural Statistics from the noted Giannini
Foundation of Agricultural Economics on the campus,
who, surprisingly, was frank to confess that some of the
deeper reaches of the mathematics were a trifle beyond
him.

In the weeks that followed, Marvin was offered a full-
time teaching post with a first year off for his research.
This he accepted. Two extracts from his thesis were published in the ensuing months in the *American Economic
Review,* the diligently selective journal of the American
Economic Association, and when these came to the attention of the Massachusetts Institute of Technology
Press, inquiries were set in motion as to publication of
the thesis itself. Marvin was more than willing, and a
year and a few months after it was accepted, it appeared
to good reviews. The MIT editor had persuaded Marvin
to a simplifying change of title; it was called *Refrigerator
Pricing: The Theoretical and Mathematical Paradigms.* For
the Marvins there was to be a major consequence.

It came when Professor Grierson back at Harvard circulated the monograph along with Marvin's *American
Economic Review* articles among his colleagues. He noted
that Marvin had been an undergraduate at Harvard and
had once been his student. There was comment from
some members of the department that Marvin's work
was unduly in the applied tradition of the University of
California; he showed excessive concern with current and

practical problems in the refrigerator industry. But eventually there was agreement: clearly he was a sterling prospect. To Marvin came a letter offering him an assistant professorship at Harvard, a tenure-track appointment. It would take Marjie away from her teaching at Berkeley, but she and Marvin, with their other intentions well in mind, were strongly disposed to accept. Marvin asked the university if he could have a year off for research before his teaching began, and it was agreed that he could.

Meanwhile in the Marvins' outside life there had been further developments.

.   .   .

In the years following his first reflections in Nevile's Court, Marvin's mind had returned frequently to the delusions of the crowd. He had read further on the dense frenzy that, in 1719, had attended the sale on the Rue Quincampoix in Paris of the stock in John Law's Compagnie d'Occident. And on that in London at the time of the South Sea Bubble. And on the manic speculation of the late 1920s in the United States. All were exercises in mass insanity; in all, the intelligence of the individual had given way to the self-reinforcing delusions of the crowd.

He looked also at the role of specific men of seeming financial genius and their capacity for communicating the errors of euphoria to others. As with the aberration of crowds, initial success bred an uncontrolled and uncontrollable excess of confidence. He was struck especially by the case of William Paterson, a Scot of no slight talent, who in the later seventeenth century had brought into being the most noted financial institution of its time and perhaps of all time — the Bank of England. From this success Paterson went on to investment and colonization in the New World. His selection of the site for his premier colony reflected a refined strategic sense: it would be Darien, situated with great precision between the two Americas and known now as the Isthmus of Panama. The Scotch, as then they were called, were entranced, and many put money into the enterprise. A sizable number were persuaded to abandon their native heather for the coarse vegetation of the tropics. Under the guidance of the founder of the Bank the colony could not fail.

Failure on that fever-ridden shore was, however, inevitable and, in the end, complete. Paterson lost his wife and child; all involved lost their money. From this disaster came humbled attitudes north of the Tweed, which helped allow of the union of Scotland and England.

There were many more such cases of individual ascent, euphoria and decline, and not negligibly in the United States. No one ever caught the imagination of the emergent American financial community more than Gentleman Jim Fisk, as he was known, the impresario, along with Daniel Drew and Jay Gould, of the Erie Rail Road. Coming from the small country town of Brattleboro, Vermont, Fisk rose to dizzying heights in the world of finance in the 1860s, taking on no less a figure than Cornelius Vanderbilt and devising an ironclad system of controlling his company by the simple device of printing such voting stock as might be necessary to serve that end. A triumphant example of the freedom of the press. Then came discovery and disillusion, the end being advanced when, in the opera house in New York that was his somewhat surprising gift to the arts, he was shot by a rival for the hand and the other and more compelling attributes of Josie Mansfield, his mistress.

Equally impressive were the glowing reputations of the men who had helped make the stock market boom of the late 1920s and their capture by their own self-esteem. There were Charles E. Mitchell and Albert H. Wiggin, heads respectively of the National City and the Chase National banks, then the nation's largest, who both had a personal and public commitment to their own special genius and who both were ignominiously sacked in the aftermath. There was Ivar Kreuger, the Swedish match king and international financier, who was similarly celebrated until the day in 1932 when he went out in Paris, bought a gun and shot himself. And there was Richard Whitney, the quintessential Harvard clubman, deeply committed to his own economic acuity, symbol of the highest standards of financial morality as expressed by the New York Stock Exchange, who passed quietly into Sing Sing after an earlier financial disaster that was brought on by the legal manufacture and sale of a Prohibition-time beverage called Jersey Lightning. In all these cases there was a lesson: find out who in any euphoric episode is the greatest hero, who is the most celebrated, and invest in his eventual fall. Or, at a minimum, be warned.

But this applied not only to individuals. Institutions could also be lifted up to and be forced down from euphoric heights. So the canal companies and railroads in the last century; so the Radio Corporation of America, the greatest speculative favorite in 1929. Such cases were not difficult to isolate and identify.

Marvin concluded that, in the current California mood, there must be modern local examples. His attention settled on the greatest of the state's financial institutions, indeed the greatest in the country at the time — the Bank of America. It was conveniently located in San Francisco, readily accessible for study, and so Marvin, with the help and support of Marjie, set out to determine how much of its present position and currently glowing prospect was based on reality, how much on the euphoria born of past success and unsupported hope. For this research the necessary material — press comment, executive speeches, interviews in the San Francisco financial community, company advertising and some discreet conversations with middle and upper management, these latter especially welcoming the interest of young scholars — was readily available.

Recalling the now distant instruction of Professor McCrimmon, Marvin set about measuring the current component of euphoria in the bank as evident in managerial optimism and resulting belief and as reflected in the price of the bank's stock. It was very substantial. With reality as 100, it was in the range of twice that figure. Born of this measurement was the method of numerical calculation that was to influence, perhaps even control, the future lives of the Marvins. One night after dinner, walking out on the terrace, the lights of Berkeley below, those of San Francisco aglow in the distance, they decided on the name — the Index of Irrational Expectations. Later, much developed and refined as to technique, it would be known and gain fame as IRAT.

As they talked that evening, the long-ago voice of Saint-Simon was heard. From the eventual losses of the many clearly come the eventual gains of the few. Why not take an affordable short position in the stock of the bank?

Marjie was eager. "You mean we should borrow stock,

sell it at current prices, and then when the price goes down, we will replace it, keeping the difference?"

"Your understanding is impeccable," said Marvin.

"A neat idea," said Marjie. "If we are willing to believe, we should be willing to risk."

Marvin demurred. Perhaps there should be further economic modeling, further testing. Also he must not now allow his attention to be diverted from his serious academic concerns.

Marjie was not similarly deterred. The next day she took BART over to San Francisco and, opening an account at Merrill Lynch, made a modest investment on her own. The ultimate return was to give her, in the favored language of the financial world, powerful leverage in influencing and, indeed, governing Marvin in the years to come.

In this family mood combining caution and supreme confidence, they packed up their still limited possessions for shipment and set out for Cambridge, Massachusetts, and their new world.

· 6 ·

THE TEXAS

TEST

IT WAS in late May that the Marvins started east. Marjie
had acquired an ample station wagon to replace the small
Toyota that had seemed to serve best on Berkeley streets.
Most of their effects having been sent on ahead, their
immediate needs — suitcases, computers, printer and a
few other items — fitted easily into the back. Celebrating
their release from academic duty, they decided to visit
Yosemite on the way, neither of them having seen it
before. The first night in the adamantly Victorian Ah-
wahnee Hotel Marjie confided news of a further probable,
if minor, distraction; she said she thought she might be
pregnant.

"At least if things work out, we can afford it," said
Marvin. "We could sell access to our index."

"If it's any good, why do we sell it?" asked Marjie,
reflecting on her secret misappropriation of its findings.
"Why let other people make money from it? Are we
running a charitable enterprise for the rich?"

"I suppose you have something there," Marvin responded amiably. "The financial genius sells advice, guidance and predictions to others because he doesn't think they're safe enough to use himself. We might be different. It will be your money, my darling, that we'll be risking."

"Why do you say risk?" asked Marjie. "I thought we had already gone beyond that small detail."

"Well, I've said it before: let's first be absolutely sure. But now tell me, which would you like, a boy or a girl?"

.　　.　　.

A couple of days later they moved out from under the towering walls of the valley and away from the downward rush of the water to seek that further assurance.

Their first serious stop was in Oklahoma City. They lodged themselves in acute discomfort in a motel amid some especially insulting scenery on the edge of the city. They then went to visit a professor of corporate organization and finance who had spent the previous year on sabbatical at Berkeley, where he had led a seminar that Marvin had occasionally attended. After some discussion, they decided to have dinner at a bar and restaurant not far from the motel.

The scene was one of extreme disorder, which grew more extreme as the evening passed. Young men in cowboy boots, Levi's and flagrantly checked shirts were drinking, eating and outshouting each other in attempted conversation. Once one kicked over a table and, after righting it, climbed on top to make a speech. It was a model of incoherence.

"They're the officers and loan committee of one of our local banks," explained the professor. "It's in the shopping mall we just passed."

"What accounts for their behavior?" asked Marvin.

"Success," said the professor. "They're channeling lots and lots of money into local oil exploration. Continental Illinois, Chase Manhattan, all the big boys, are using their expertise."

"They seem to be enjoying it" was all Marvin could think of to say.

The next day, while Marjie stayed in bed with a bout of morning sickness, Marvin, representing himself as an interested scholar and writer, visited the bank. He talked to the officer in charge of public relations, who provided him with institutional literature and a file of Xeroxed newspaper clippings. He was introduced to a couple of men, dressed in the style of the country, who had come in for loans, and they spoke with enthusiasm of what the bank was doing for oil exploration in the Permian Basin, of which Marvin had not previously heard.

That evening back at the motel he chatted in the bar with a lean, rather disconsolate man who, it turned out, had recently been a loan officer at the bank. Hearing of Marvin's interest, he talked volubly and somewhat alcoholically of its operations. He had been given the sack for, he said, being "too much on the conservative side. I brought up the matter of risk and repayment." Evidently impressed by Marvin's willingness to listen, he arranged a meeting the next morning for a further chat, at which time he offered some examples of loans made and passed on to the "big fellows" in Chicago, New York and Seattle and his thoughts on the collateral.

Later that day, back in their room, Marvin put together a very rough Index of Irrational Expectations for the bank. It was several times reality, perhaps in the neighborhood of 400.

To both the Marvins it was evident that, were it possible, they should take a strong short position in the stock of the bank. Marjie again reflected on her decision to act on the admittedly milder IRAT showing on the Bank of America.

.   .   .

Their pleasure in their findings in Oklahoma City was mitigated somewhat by the blistering early summer weather and Marjie's continued morning sickness. They thought of going directly to New England, but with many weeks still ahead of them before they needed to be in Cambridge, they stuck to plan and went on to Texas. They knew from their reading that that state was then in an especially euphoric mood.

Arriving in Austin, the spacious site of the University of Texas and the state Capitol, they stayed with a friend from Harvard days, now a rising figure in the Lyndon Baines Johnson School of Public Affairs. The first night they were there, there was a small welcoming party around the swimming pool. The economist for one of the larger Austin banks had intruded upon an otherwise scholarly gathering, and he made his presence evident by declaiming vigorously on the glowing outlook for the local residential and commercial real estate market.

"Austin is the best prospect in the country," he said. "Better even than Dallas or Houston. There is nothing like it in all the United States. We are the intellectual heart of the Sunbelt. We're about to become a world-class high-tech center. The Japanese will be coming here to learn." He went on to describe the real estate developments planned or under way, especially mentioning those of two of the most distinguished figures of the Texas political past, a former governor and former Secretary of the Treasury in Washington and a former lieutenant governor.

"They bring to the real estate business the wisdom and the experience, the imagination and the enthusiasm, of all their years in public service. A wonderful thing for them and for our whole community."

Most of the guests listened less attentively than did Marvin; they clearly had heard too much of it before. His ear, which was already carefully attuned, detected more than a trace of the optimism and commitment that justify their own conclusion.

The following morning, with the quiet approval of his host, he and Marjie set out to establish an IRAT on the real estate operation they had been discussing. That the men involved were of excellent local reputation could not eliminate the possibility of error building as ever on its own hopes. After a couple of days of investigation, including several interviews and a look at plans for a spectacular housing development in the near neighborhood — architecture with size compensating for horror but saved thoughtfully from public view by the vast acreage of surrounding scrubland — they found that the index rating was clear. It was lower than that of the Oklahoma bank, but the prospect for an eventual return to reality was nonetheless grim. Warning their host in a restrained way of their finding, they went north to Dallas.

．　　．　　．

It was a long, hot drive. A Texas governor once observed that anyone driving at the speed limit in his state did not

arrive. Eventually, however, the city appeared in the distance — lean, geometric towers in close agglomeration,
shimmering in the sun.

"Why," Marjie asked, "with so much acreage does so
much have to be jammed into so little space? Does everyone have to be within walking distance of Neiman-Mar-
cus?"

"Texans don't ever walk," said Marvin. "It's the real
estate industry. Spread the city out over a few more
square miles and look what you would do to inner-city
values."

Remembering the discomforts and urgent traffic din of
the motel in Oklahoma, they housed themselves more
agreeably in the excellent local Hilton.

.   .   .

The three weeks that Marvin devoted to Dallas that summer were among the most instructive of his academic
career. Introducing himself, not implausibly, as a young
Harvard professor interested in the economic prospects
for Texas, he interviewed senior bank officials, including
those of the RepublicBank Corporation and InterFirst,
two giants that would eventually be merged. Also the
top management of two of the more expansive savings
and loan associations — the thrifts, as somewhat imagi-
natively they are called. And he met several of the leading
commercial real estate developers, whose soaring structures were so wonderfully evident to the eye.

Between the interviews and in the evenings, he and
Marjie devoured the newspaper accounts, annual reports,
company brochures, Xeroxed speeches and other published and unpublished materials and, laboring over their

computers, brought to bear the tests that measured the extent to which success reinforced delusion to sustain credulity.

Not before had they seen the expected elements so powerfully present. A certainty of gain proceeding from unchallenged self-esteem — the natural reward of initiative and vision. Pessimism rejected as a denial of personality. Illusion reinforced by shared illusions. Certainty reinforced by shared certainty.

But here theology also entered. To have doubts was to repudiate the established tenets. The good man must have faith in Texas, faith in America, faith in the free enterprise system and faith in oil, the energy source on which depended the very mobility of a people by whom other than petroleum-powered movement had been forgotten. But especially faith in Texas. Doubt belonged to the cold and obsolescent North, to the lesser breeds beyond the sun.

For the banks and savings and loan associations there was a yet further support to faith, more substantial even than the established beliefs. This was the United States government. It effectively guaranteed the deposits in the banks and the thrifts; if anything went wrong, the depositors' money would still be there and theirs. From this came the certainty that no really large financial institution would be allowed to fail. So business could expand, risks could be taken, without the threat or thought of a devastating end. Free enterprise but with the ultimate and benign support of socialism.

Marvin and Marjie, as they drew up the relevant indices for two banks, two big savings and loan associations and three large real estate developers, could not but feel that they had encountered the ultimate justification of their system. Never was the controlling role of euphoria so obvious. Never so obvious was the money that might be made by going short in the stock of the large institutions they were studying.

And there was another, equally impressive lesson.

This came one day when one of the bankers invited the Marvins to lunch. He was a short, rotund man, bald, with a markedly forthcoming air, and both Marvin and Marjie found themselves attracted to him almost at once. The club to which they went was high in an enormously tall office building. In contrast with the nearly impenetrable gloom of the Harvard Club in New York, to which Marvin had once been invited, the general aspect was bright, even cheerful. No one at the surrounding tables appeared to be of the Texas prototype. That, Marvin had always supposed, was tall, lean, sun-hardened, much like the models in the cigarette ads. These men were full-chinned and affable in manner and if not obese, then comfortably compact. The Marvins' host took charge of the conversation.

"I hear you-all think we're havin' quite a speculative fling down here. Someone I met was talkin' about you th'other day."

"I haven't said so, but it does seem possible, I admit."

"Your instinct, if that's what you call it, is extremely good. And there isn't a thing that can be done about it."

"Why not?"

"It's just a lot bigger than any of us. A lot bigger than I am. And it's a very, very practical matter. If I didn't believe in Texas, in the future of oil, the future of the energy industry as you call it, in the fillin' up of all that office space you can see out there, I would be treated as if I had a bad case of the leprosy. Or anyhow acute halitosis. I wouldn't have any business at all. Not when word got around that we were a bunch of sour mouths. Not lendin' like the rest."

"Isn't it a bit dangerous?" ventured Marvin.

"Sure is. Very, very dangerous. But what's the alternative? Our Mr. Sam said it about the Congress: 'You-all get along by goin' along.' You probably die later. Better than hittin' the coffin right now." He went on to enlarge on his thesis.

The point, Marvin thought later as they waited for the elevator, could not be more clear. The dementia that they measured could be individual, as in the case of William Paterson, Ivar Kreuger, Gentleman Jim Fisk or the young men at the Oklahoma bank. Or it could be institutional, as in the case of the Bank of America and the banks they had just studied. Or it could be collective, as with the crowds in the Rue Quincampoix in the eighteenth century or on Wall Street before the crash of 1929. But there was a further possibility, as here in Texas: it could be compelled. There was no choice but to conform, march in lock step to the inevitable collapse.

．　．　．

Eventually and somewhat reluctantly Marvin and Marjie rejoined their station wagon, loaded their luggage, including now a large package of computer printouts, and headed for what was soon to be home. They considered going to Houston; this, however, they assured themselves (and were assured) would be more of the same.

They stopped for a couple of days in Washington,

where they were joined for dinner by another economist friend from Harvard who had come over from Baltimore, where he was now serving time, as he saw it, at Johns Hopkins University. He asked what they had been doing in Dallas, and they told him that they were looking at the Sunbelt boom as manifested in the great Texas banks, thrifts and real estate operations. He, in turn, described the wave of initiative and optimism that, with deregulation, was already coming upon the Maryland thrifts. The prospect was very attractive; something really exciting could be under way. Marvin and Marjie discussed the matter that night at the Hay-Adams Hotel, where, in a further burst of self-indulgence, they had taken a large room looking out on the White House. Should they warn their friend by showing him some of their earlier measurements? He was clearly about to be caught up in some bamboozlement. They concluded that it was too soon; later on, an IRAT might prove very interesting. So, after strolling through the National Gallery and the Smithsonian, visiting, as Berkeley protocol required, with Congressman Dellums and looking in on a Senate debate that was evidently engrossing to all six of the members on the floor, they continued on their way to Cambridge.

· · ·

Paying a more than modest reward to find housing that was still under rent control, a well-established technique for evading the city rent regulations, the Marvins moved into an unfashionably situated but large and entirely comfortable apartment on Prescott Street behind the Faculty Club, a block only from the Yard. Marvin had extra phone lines installed, explaining to a neighbor who expressed surprise that, as an economist, he needed access to assorted data banks.

He was given a small, slightly arid office at the university and, at his own expense, hired the intelligent secretary of a recently retired professor, who took pleasure in informing him as to the more superficial intricacies of university existence. She seemed to think it natural when he told her he hoped she would respect his desire for a certain reticence regarding his strictly personal affairs. It was only later that she learned that he was alluding to quite innocent financial operations.

Marvin attended his first department meeting in late September, was warmly welcomed and warmly congratulated on his work on refrigerator pricing.

"A theoretical and mathematical gem," one colleague commented. Professor Grierson was equally gracious.

Marvin indicated his intention to extend the analysis in future years to freezers and perhaps also commercial refrigeration. Thinking to protect himself against any rumors that might circulate as to his outside activities, he indicated that he had some interest in making a model of investment prospects in various other industries. No one paid attention.

. . .

One day while getting a quick bit of lunch at the Wursthaus, an ancient rendezvous in Harvard Square, Marvin saw Professor McCrimmon idling over coffee at an adjacent table. On his way out, he stopped to shake hands and tell him that he had just come on from California.

"Don't I remember you from Oxford?" asked McCrimmon. "Are you getting tenure?"

"So I'm advised," said Marvin.

"Often the first step to senility," said McCrimmon with the air of someone making an original point. "It usually comes very soon thereafter."

"My hope is to do a little better than that, sir," said Marvin.

"You will be the exception if you do," said Mc-Crimmon. "But I seem to remember that you had some other career plans in mind. Reforming the Republic?"

"You told me to wait until I had tenure."

"Very wise," said McCrimmon.

Marvin did have other plans in mind. They concerned not public affairs but private money. Marjie had recently confessed to her Bank of America speculation, and Marvin had decided that he couldn't let her go on alone.

· 7 ·

MONEY

As he got into it, Marvin found the making of money surprisingly agreeable. At the back of their spacious, old-fashioned apartment was a small but not entirely unpleasant room; in academically more expansive days it had evidently housed a maid. This they converted into an office. From a course in computer science at the university they recruited a versatile young technician who promised complete discretion. A brokerage house on State Street in Boston was brought into their service, as also the local Cambridge Trust Company. An accounting firm in the neighboring suburb of Waltham, felicitously called Peck, Peck & Peck, took over their record keeping and tax preparation and, rather to its surprise, soon found they had become one of its larger clients.

The Marvins' operations were astringently conservative. Only if a common stock or other investment instrument had a safely high IRAT did they take a short position — as ever, they borrowed the stock and sold it at the current high price, replacing it later at the bargain prices then prevailing. Euphoria, to attract them, had to be far advanced and building relentlessly against the inevitable day of truth. If the index value was very low — well below reality — they bought. There was then need to wait for the correction; here again, given their care in the construction of the index, the result was certain. Long positions, however, lacked the dramatic inevitability of advanced euphoria. When the latter was present, the eventual collapse was built in, programmed and rewardingly, resoundingly complete.

At first they were somewhat limited by the amount of Marjie's inheritance, although that was not insignificant. After their initial successes, however, their resources expanded and so did their working capital. Two of the largest Boston banks were then brought to their assistance, and, while avowing caution in the best Boston tradition, they provided a very satisfactory line of credit with which yet larger positions could be taken.

In time, the work fell into a near routine. Care and judgment were still required in the identification and assessment of euphoria and the construction of the indices, even though, with experience, they found the manifestations of euphoria reaching on to insanity increasingly clear. Once or twice a month, sometimes more often, Marvin took the Eastern shuttle to New York to seek out new forms of delusion and self-delusion. There he attended the scheduled briefings of investment analysts that concentrated on some especially unpromising and thus promising prospects. These sessions were never decisive in themselves, but they did supplement and affirm the indices that, from external claims and internal evidence, were being created.

Marvin's absences from Cambridge were little noticed;

Harvard professors, and especially in economics, are known to be greatly addicted to travel. It was said that in earlier and more socially committed times members of the economics department had regularly held faculty meetings on the Federal Express as it went from South Station to Washington; thus, purportedly, had the message of Maynard Keynes been taken to the capital. To the extent that anyone noticed that Marvin was away, it was assumed that he was pursuing his field work on refrigerator pricing.

.   .   .

In January of his first academic year at Harvard there was a brief interruption in their routine. Marjie went to Brigham and Women's Hospital for two days, where she was delivered of twins — a son and a daughter. It seemed an almost casual thing; her mother, when giving birth to Marjie, had been kept in a maternity hospital for a full week. Congratulations came from Marvin's colleagues at almost the same time that he got word he had been accorded tenure.

The department had voted it with only two or three dissenting voices. One member had detected what he thought to be a flaw in some of Marvin's equations depicting the component cost effect of the refrigerator line he was analyzing; a second deplored the unduly applied character of his work; yet another drew attention, as often before, to the department's continuing failure to find women and minority candidates.

In accordance with university practice, an *ad hoc* committee composed of outside scholars unprejudiced by close personal acquaintance was called together to pass on Marvin's promotion. Its members assembled in University Hall, one of the loveliest of Charles Bulfinch's creations; discussed Marvin's work, his papers on refrigeration price theory being in folders before them; adjourned for lunch and returned to give their approval. That Marvin's writing was somewhat on the practical side was noted; no one, however, questioned its technical competence. It contributed usefully to agreement that the names recommended for the committee had come from Professor Grierson, who had suggested academic figures both informed on, and impressed by, Marvin's earlier achievements. Since no one knew, no one was influenced by the fact that some of Professor Montgomery Marvin's energies were now devoted to his becoming personally very rich.

.   .   .

As in Berkeley the months passed into years. As in Berkeley in earlier times, Ronald Reagan — now, of course, President Ronald Reagan — was a presence in the community. Even some of the more theoretically committed members of the faculty found themselves asked about the budget priorities of David Stockman, the monetarist magic of Professor Milton Friedman, the now compelling doctrine that the rich were not working because they had too little money, the poor because they had too much. And about the Laffer Curve. Especially about the Laffer Curve.

This economic formulation of high personal importance to the Marvins held that when no taxes are levied, no revenue accrues to the government. An undoubted truth. And if taxes are so high that they absorb all income, nothing can be collected from the distraught, starving and otherwise nonfunctional citizenry. Also almost certainly true. Between those two points a freehand curve, engagingly unsupported by evidence, showed the point where higher taxes would mean less revenue. According to accepted legend, the original curve had been drawn on a paper napkin, possibly toilet paper, and some critics of deficient imagination held that the paper could have been better put to its intended use. Marvin and Marjie were not, however, tempted to such a conclusion. There was 'good reason.

As Laffer's analysis appealed deeply to Mr. Reagan, so it did to the Marvins, for it went far to protect their developing design. By substantially reducing levies on the top income brackets, it left them with a great deal more usable cash than would previously have been the case. The purpose of such a reduction, it was said, was to expand the effort, initiative and other energies of the rich, and nowhere in the Republic did it serve those ends more admirably than in the large, paper-strewn, slightly shabby apartment on Prescott Street, with its inescapable aspect of use and overcrowding. Whether, as promised by Mr. Reagan's acolytes, it also enhanced the efficient production of goods and services was another question. It did mean that the money that now came in to the Marvins did not pass relentlessly on to Washington. However unintended the result, Marvin and Marjie were prime beneficiaries of, as it was to be called, the Reagan revolution.

· · ·

The Marvins did not separate themselves in any ostentatious way from the Cambridge social scene. Entertaining in their apartment, alongside the computers, the printer, the printouts, the telephones and the twins, was difficult. However, the Faculty Club was almost across the street, and there they took visitors and friends and their aging parents when in town on obligatory trips to see the grandchildren. On occasion, they hired a room on an upper floor of the club for small parties. These were not enjoyed; in Cambridge, as elsewhere in university life, it is recognized, sensibly, that social intercourse is not meant to be enjoyed; it is very often a ritual to be endured in the interest of academic repute.

Marvin resumed his association with Dunster House, went for house dinners and marked his calendar to remind himself that he should lunch there at least once a month. He taught a course that centered on the refrigerator industry — Advanced Econometric Analyses of Selected Durable Product Prices; it was highly regarded and had a respectable if still modest attendance. He also took part with two colleagues, one older and one just out of graduate school, in a workshop on the same subject. At Harvard, as at other universities, attendance at courses in advanced analytical theory and methodology cannot be guaranteed, but, as Professor McCrimmon had earlier suggested, a workshop that promises the presence of participant colleagues ensures against the mild personal embarrassment from scheduling a seminar or lecture course and having no one come.

With tenure secure, the Marvins now ventured on a slightly more active political life. Marjie, out of her long Canadian commitment to improving the political manners, morals and governance of the United States, took the lead. In no way did this reveal their ultimate design; in Cambridge not to be so involved was in some measure to be delinquent. In 1980, in Berkeley, they had reacted with decently restrained enthusiasm to the presidential campaign of Edward Kennedy. Now in 1984 they openly supported Walter Mondale, a preference that in this community was not entirely exceptional. One day in the autumn of that year Marvin saw a small crowd looking with amazement at a newly parked car on the university road back of Littauer Center. The focus of attention was a bumper sticker supporting the re-election of Ronald Reagan.

Along with a group of aspiring young women from the Harvard Business School, Marjie interested herself in a new project called the Executive Gender Survey — EXEGES, as it was known. This, with modest and reticent financial support from the Marvins, examined the proportion of women employed in executive positions in the Fortune 500 corporations with an eye to increasing their number. In future years it would demand more of the Marvins' time and energy and a bit more of their money.

· · ·

The Marvins' stock market operations remained, at most, only a faint rumor. In keeping these activities relatively quiet, they were greatly aided by the local social life, that centering on Harvard and the Massachusetts Institute of Technology.

By long custom, social discourse in Cambridge is intended to impart and only rarely to obtain information. People talk; it is not expected that anyone will listen. A respectful show of attention is all that is required until the listener takes over in his or her turn. No one has ever been known to repeat what he or she has heard at a party or other social gathering, only what he or she has said. There may then be further enlargement on the skill and emphasis with which the compelling point has been made; to this, also, no one has ever been known to pay attention.

This folk rite served the Marvins well. One occasion was especially sharp in their memory. It was autumn. All countries are known to have their particular season. In England it is spring. In France, in the French countryside, it is the long summer when Paris is empty. In Switzerland it is winter, and in the United States, and notably in New England, it is the autumn. The founding fathers, in their genius, set these golden months aside for elections and election campaigning, while succeeding generations of possibly lesser imagination have reserved them for football.

Late one lovely afternoon in 1984, after a football game they had not attended, Marvin and Marjie drove along the Charles amid an explosion of richly burnished colors to the neighboring town of Newton. They had been invited for cocktails and a buffet dinner at the house of one of the more justly celebrated deans of the university, who made a special point of getting to know the younger members of the faculty.

The game that afternoon had been won by Harvard; the assemblage was ebullient; the conversations, more precisely the monologues, were resonant. Marvin, according to his custom, took refuge with his plate in a moderately quiet corner slightly out of the way. There he was joined by a fellow professor with whom he had a nodding acquaintance, a neighbor from a few blocks away who was prominent in the field of biotechnics.

To Marvin's discomfort, his companion opened the conversation by saying, "I hear that you're involved with the stock market these days. Making some money?"

"Where did you hear that?" Marvin asked. His voice, he was afraid, sounded more concerned than surprised.

His companion, somewhat exceptionally, responded to the question. "My brother. I think he met you once. He's in the financial purlieus, as they say or don't say. He had lunch at the downtown Harvard Club the other day, and a guy from one of the brokerage houses asked if, by any chance, he knew you. Said you were a good customer. Or is it client?"

Marvin resisted the temptation to deny. Denial, when the eventual and unwelcome truth comes out, as so often it does, adds to the weight of the original accusation the further, heavier one of being known as a liar. It suggests that the aberration was sufficiently serious to call for a cover-up. This was something which he had noticed was little understood these days in Mr. Reagan's Washington.

"After all, I'm an economist," he managed to interject. "I need to put my ideas occasionally to the test."

"I got the impression you were putting them to a fairly substantial one."

Changing the subject slightly, Marvin said, "I wonder if that broker should have been talking that way."

"Probably a bit slurred mentally after the second martini. It gets that way down there on State Street at noon. It's certainly not an academic tendency. I'm told the Faculty Club didn't used to serve even beer."

He continued: "My brother got the impression that you're a determined pessimist — the opposite of everything they advise. He was rather blunt about it. Said you were a good guide to what not to do. In the financial world this, he thinks, is rightly a time of good feeling, optimism. I hope I'm not being too candid in telling you all this."

Marvin started to speak, but the other man didn't give up. "Suppose you're successful, as I hope you will be. Aren't you using your knowledge and research as a Harvard professor to make money for yourself? That's the kind of thing we people in the applied sciences have to be pretty careful about. You probably saw McCrimmon's interview on that in the *Globe* the other day."

"My own research is in the field of durable goods pricing — refrigerators and the like. The opportunities aren't great."

His friend passed over the point and enlarged at some length on the conflict between publicly supported research and professorial self-interest.

By now most of the early and a few of the very late arrivals were leaving. Marvin went to collect Marjie, who was dominating the conversation in a small group of reluctant listeners. She seemed to be telling of the interesting early psychic tendencies of their daughter, Laura.

On the way home Marvin told her what he had heard about their financial operations; they would have to be braced for further discussion of their affairs. He wondered if the consequences might not be less than they feared. Idiosyncratic pessimism would surely not be taken seriously: just a professorial deviation from the more reputable assumption of rational expectations. More to the point, perhaps all criticism might be silenced if their returns were shared in a modest way with the university.

Marvin went on to suggest that they send some kind

of rebuke to the brokerage house; certainly they could ask for a little more discretion.

"I have a better idea," said Marjie. "Let's just shift our business to someone else."

Marvin agreed.

For the distinguished company in question this would be no minor loss in the years to come. The Marvins' operations were soon to be on a scale about which, as regards commissions, every brokerage house is known to dream.

. 8 .

CORRECTION

AROUND THE MIDDLE of 1985, the Marvins' operations took a different form. Previously they had calculated the IRAT as it applied to individual corporations, but now in the mid-eighties came a new situation. The financial world not alone of New York but also of London, Hong Kong and Tokyo — literally the whole world of merchantable securities — was turning in their favor. Irrationality was becoming general; euphoria was becoming endemic and universal. Securities prices across the board were going up. And because prices were going up, people were buying with a view to grabbing some of the gain, thus sending them up yet further. The Marvins watched the Dow Jones Average; tradition has its claims. At the end of 1984, the Dow industrials had been at 1211.57; at the end of 1985, they were to be at 1546.67; and twelve months later at 1895.95.

So the Marvins changed course. They began to run index ratings at random — from General Electric to General Dynamics, General Mills, General Foods and IBM. From all came the same result: euphoria was no longer special but general. Over the whole securities market from common stock to high-risk, or junk, bonds the readings were in the same direction. The powerful vested interest that develops in optimism was everywhere evident. Who, if he is getting rich, would believe otherwise than in the solidity and benignity of the forces that are the cause?

Marvin remembered another passage from Walter Bagehot's *Lombard Street:* "Every great crisis reveals the excessive speculations of many houses which no one before suspected . . ." This ancient wisdom IRAT was now affirming. Euphoria was now being enhanced by an exfoliation of mutual funds and closed-end investment trusts. The latter harked back to the great promotions of the 1920s — to Goldman Sachs and the Goldman Sachs Trading Corporation, which in 1929 created the Shenandoah Corporation, which in turn created the Blue Ridge Corporation. None of these firms toiled to produce goods or render services; all were brought into being to bring a great and special wisdom to speculative success. All came to nothing, went nearly to nothing. Now, in but slightly different form, history was repeating itself. Program trading, as it was called, was bringing the more exacting intelligence of the computer to bear on imagined market opportunity. Portfolio insurance was created to protect the investor from the losses that almost no one expected. Index trading — investment for the rewards from a general increase in values free from the need for scrutiny of individual companies — was a new and greatly favored development. Option trading — not the

purchase of a stock but the purchase of the right to purchase — was reducing dramatically the claim on personal
resources or credit while still allowing participation in the
assured rewards from assuredly increasing values.

The excitement penetrated even the ivied walls. Students emerging from the Harvard Business School had
once headed for a steady, unspectacular and not unre-
munerative ascent through the great corporate bureau-
cracies. Now, along with some from what had been an
undergraduate preoccupation with economics, athletics
or comparative literature, they went in numbers to Wall
Street. There they took part in mergers and acquisitions,
leveraged buyouts and the restructuring of the resulting
firms, all for a hitherto unimagined personal gain. In this
service they worked hand in hand with former fellow
students from the Harvard Law School who were re-
jecting the attractions of politics or public service or the
spiritual rewards of *pro bono* law for the more immediate
charm of large pay and, no one doubted, exceptionally
long hours of hideous toil.

.   .   .

Marvin was sought out late one afternoon at Prescott
Street by a young man just out of the Business School;
he had been in one of Marvin's undergraduate courses
and had gone on to join the staff of the great investment
house of Drexel Burnham Lambert. In strict confidence,
he put to his former professor a series of questions on
the refrigerator business; he said that a takeover of a major
producer in the industry was in prospect, the raider operating behind the façade of a new company called, ap-
propriately, Cold International, Inc. Marvin, always

helpful where students and ex-students were concerned, gave a full court account of the pricing practices and competitive exposure of the firm being sought. He was thanked effusively. Later it occurred to him that he was the unwitting recipient of possibly rewarding and indubitably illegal inside information. In keeping with his professional principles, he avoided any thought of acting on it.

He and Marjie did, however, act on the general upward movement of the market, and on a scale larger than they had ever earlier considered. They borrowed heavily on their now eagerly extended lines of credit. And, as the indices showed the market going on to yet higher levels of assured and vested optimism, they resorted also to index trading, the centerpiece of this operation being the Standard & Poor's 500. They stretched to their now ample limit the sale of index futures, which, they noted with satisfaction, required only a 10 percent down payment against the prospect of a 100 percent return or better.

. . .

None of this was wholly without thought as to worst-case consequence. "What happens if a Harvard professor goes bankrupt?" Marjie asked over breakfast one morning. "How many professors have gone into Chapter 11?"

Marvin, having put aside *The Wall Street Journal,* was deep in computer printouts. "It *has* happened to professors," he replied. "Some were involved in the 1929 crash. At Yale there was Irving Fisher, our mentor in fact, the inventor of index numbers. You've heard of him: the most innovative economist of his time. In early 1929, he concluded that stocks had reached a new, permanently high plateau and went badly broke on the error. The university helped to bail him out; it bought his house and let him rent it back as long as he wanted. I wonder if Harvard would be so thoughtful."

"They wouldn't want this apartment. Anyway, like Fisher, we always have tenure."

"Sure, we're safe. If tenure protects socialists and communists, it has to protect failed capitalists. We aren't into anything people here think really serious, like sex. But I must go, I have a class."

. . .

The Marvins, such thoughts notwithstanding, did not lack confidence. In 1986, Marvin read first of the sudden descent of Dennis Levine and then of that of Ivan Boesky, two world-class exploiters of inside information. He thought again of his own higher principles as expressed on that refrigerator takeover. A few years before, at a large meeting of deeply attentive securities analysts at an investment house in midtown New York, he had sat near Boesky. An eager flow of men and an occasional woman of his generation had come up to shake hands and exchange a word or two with the erstwhile financial genius. *Darshan*, the Hindu touch of the great.

Wall Street has its own measure of worth, and Marvin had come to know it well. The measure is not rectitude, not public virtue, not personal saintliness, not intelligence, not even personal hygiene, though that is a commendable thing after a long day in the shirt-sleeved trading room. The measure is simple and inescapable: it is dollars having been earned and being accumulated.

As often before, Marvin listened that day in New York

to an appreciation of the limitless and unalloyed future of a deeply questionable enterprise, this one involving the esoterica of a new microchip. He felt a moment of encouragement. Money was the scorecard for this committed community. And by its standards, he was by no means insignificant. It was only that his score was not publicly known.

There was another feeling of personal approval in weeks to come when Mr. Boesky was taken in hand by the federal authorities. "We have the advantage," he said to Marjie, "that we are within the law."

"Don't be so solemn," said Marjie. "If they find out what we intend, they will change the law." Marjie often spoke better than she knew.

. . .

In November 1986, the market reacted adversely to the Boesky scandal, as it was called. The Dow dropped 56 points, and the Marvins took some profits. Their indices, however, showed that optimism was still largely undiminished. And in succeeding months, it was greatly enhanced. The Marvins bet against it with all their resources, including all that they could borrow. It was costing them money — interest — to stay, but they could not doubt that the end was coming. They knew it especially that next September, when for a large number of stocks the IRAT reached a full 200. By simple calculation, the optimism thus accounted for nearly half the total value of those securities. The Marvins' day seemed near.

. . .

October 19, 1987, dawned like any other Monday. The stock market had fallen sharply at the end of the previous week, and Marvin was alert to the possibility of further trouble, but his academic work came first. He breakfasted in an atypically unhurried fashion, and after an hour or so of diligent preparation — review of his notes from earlier years, a glance over the assigned reading, a quick look at his own published papers on the subject as a reminder — he went off to teach his class. Harvard courses are given on Mondays, Wednesdays and Fridays or on Tuesdays, Thursdays and Saturdays. Devoted teachers choose the Monday, Wednesday, Friday regime, for Saturday classes are either poorly attended or, as in recent times, not given at all. Marvin, conscientious as was his nature, followed the Monday, Wednesday routine and, aided by the assignment of his own book — a greatly approved university practice — was able to deal with the theoretical and mathematical aspects of price and production analysis for refrigerators and other closely related products well within the limits of the number of lectures allowed for a year. (Just as it is understood at the modern university that any idea can be compressed or expanded into fifty-five minutes, so it is also believed that all knowledge on a subject can be covered in either thirteen or twenty-six weeks.)

His lecture over, Marvin strolled to Harvard Square to fill a prescription at the University Health Services Pharmacy for Marjie to give to one of the children; the twins were enrolled in the local day care center, but today Laura was ill. On a side street off Massachusetts Avenue, the main thoroughfare of the city, he passed a small brokerage office, not one he had ever patronized. He noticed a

large and, as he looked more closely, rather tensely
preoccupied crowd within. Curiosity combined with self-
interest, and he entered. Almost immediately he encountered his friend from biotechnics, the man who had once
seemed a threat to the confidential character of the Marvins' operations. The professor's eyes were glued to the
Quotron.

"What's happening?" Marvin asked.

"A correction," said his colleague, his attention un-
diverted. "A really major correction," he added by way
of emphasis. "Everything is off. IBM. GE. 3M . . ."

"Are you involved?"

"A bit. My brother, I think I told you about him. We
just talked — took me half an hour to get through. That's
why I'm here. He said it's a major correction."

Marvin watched for a while. Prices were in a downward slide, each quotation below the last. On the way
out he met Professor Grierson.

"I hear it's very bad," said Grierson.

"A major correction," said Marvin, falling easily into
the approved reference.

. . .

Back at home, he got on the telephone. Even with his
special line he had trouble making connections. Getting
through, he got the confirmation he sought; he was one
of the few not phoning in to sell.

Marjie was still busy with her sick child. A sore throat,
an inflamed tonsil. The Health Services had prescribed an
antibiotic, which Laura was taking under extreme protest.

To ease matters, Marvin strolled across the street to
the Faculty Club and sat down at the long table for a very

late lunch. News of what was happening in the stock market had naturally not penetrated, but the conversation, oddly enough, was on financial matters. Ever since students had erected shanties in the Yard urging divestment of university holdings in firms doing business in South Africa, such divestment had been a recurring topic for discussion. A professor of romance languages was wondering if, given the general economic prospect, the university could really afford it. Others thought it could. The debate was lively. McCrimmon expressed doubt that an academic institution should own any common stocks at all.

.   .   .

One of Marvin's rules of behavior was never to allow the daily fluctuations in the market to intrude on his thoughts. The Index of Irrational Expectations, with its built-in numbers telling when to sell and when to buy, was designed to avoid such tension. But to all such rules there are exceptions. After lunch Marvin telephoned Marjie to tell her where he was going and took the subway into Boston. He got off at Park Street and, surprised at his own calm, walked down into the financial district to the offices of the largest of the brokerage houses now handling their business.

At Harvard Marvin was a professor; here on State Street he was, in a modest and circumspect way, a presence, even a personage. Although he had to identify himself to an attendant, when he did, he was guided to an inner sanctum for financially significant clients. Here a dozen or so had come to observe the market in comfortable decorum. Outside the room there was a marked aspect of tension and movement; inside, there was a superficial sense of calm. It occurred to Marvin that it was a mark of the really rich that they could lose their money with seeming dignity. On further observation, he concluded that he could not have been more wrong. After noting with well-concealed satisfaction that the market had taken and was still taking a drop for which even IRAT had scarcely prepared him, he turned his attention with apparent casualness to his fellow viewers.

There could be no doubt as to their suffering. A woman across the room dabbed her eyes surreptitiously with a handkerchief. A man not far away, faking the need for shade from the dim lights overhead, periodically covered his eyes with his hands. From others there were no such revealing gestures, only grim concentration on the Translux overhead. Occasionally someone would go out and return — perhaps another order to sell. Worst of all was the word that the ticker was running two hours late. A terrible present with the inescapable suggestion of a worse future.

Marvin, his eyes on the changing figures, saw himself getting richer, and literally by the minute. He wondered if, in contrast with those other faces, his was concealing the inner truth.

Eventually the trading for the day came to an end. Marvin walked out behind an attenuated figure in a blue jacket and grey flannels who stopped him as they passed into the larger outside room where the proletarian investors were making their way, some in all too obvious grief, to the door.

"You're out at Harvard, aren't you?"

"Yes," said Marvin, "have we met?"

"I was on your Department Visiting Committee the year you were appointed. I'm the class of '54. What do you make of this terrible business — as an economics professor, I mean? Were you in it for much?"

"A significant correction," said Marvin, varying his reference. Then he hedged: "But I wasn't too badly hurt. What about you?"

"It was bad. I hope someone in Washington comes out tomorrow — should be Reagan himself — with a reassuring statement. Stress that the economy is fundamentally sound."

"That was what President Hoover said several times after the 1929 crash," volunteered Marvin.

"We can't hear those fundamental truths too often. Let me ask you again, what about this business today?"

"A very fundamental correction," said Marvin.

His companion seemed to agree. Shoulders rather hunched, he disappeared into the crowd. After a moment's thought, Marvin took a taxi back to Prescott Street.

· 9 ·

INTERLUDE

By the evening of Black Monday the Marvins were indeed very rich. In the newspapers in the week that followed, there would be mention of the thousands who had lost millions. Even the infinitely distinguished men who managed Harvard's portfolio would be assessing their losses on that strenuous day, one in which they had sold heavily but, like so many, not quite soon enough. Later there would be stories of other large investors, also blessed with presumed acumen, who had rushed too late to escape. And of the myriad of small investors who had tried similarly to get out but for whom the telephone lines were blocked. There would be no mention whatever of the young, quiet, bearded, somewhat retiring Harvard professor, the admitted authority on the econometrics of the refrigerator industry, whose gains were from all their losses.

Americans, by nature, invest in success. But recurrent failure is also endemic in their economic life and system.

How great the reward of those who recognize this and act to their own advantage. Such was the Marvins' fortune.

. . .

Exceptionally, in the weeks after the crash, Marvin slighted slightly his teaching; his course assistant, an accomplished mathematician and econometrician, even took over a class or two. The indices were recalculated to reflect the new market conditions; they now showed a negative stock market valuation for a significant number of securities. Euphoria had given way to net pessimism. The Marvins moved to a long position, again with maximum leverage — leverage from borrowing on the vast resources with which the crash had endowed them.

They also observed with interest the reaction of the financial world to what had happened. At all cost the sanctity of the securities markets had to be protected. As God cannot be of any evil, Mary of any even venial sin, so markets cannot be thought to incorporate any tendency to inherent error — not the New York Stock Exchange, not the American Stock Exchange, not even the distant bourses of Tokyo and Hong Kong. One cannot harbor doubts as to the essential virtue of the greatest of free enterprise institutions. To this end, Secretaries of the Treasury of the recent past, lamented and unlamented; retired statesmen, some dubious, some revered but all still seeking public voice; and the more compulsively articulate of the nation's great business executives joined in a costly advertisement in *The New York Times* to relieve the market of blame. The federal budget, then deeply in deficit as it had been long before, was held to be the principal precipitating factor in the crash. Not Wall Street but Washington was at fault. The government, accordingly, should move to cut expenditures and raise taxes, preferably those which did not impinge too seriously on the signers of the advertisement.

Then in the ensuing months diverse commissions were impaneled to identify a deeper, more persuasive cause. It was decided that the casino adjuncts of the market — program trading, index trading, option trading and portfolio insurance, all so recently hailed as the innovations of the age — were to blame. Had these ancillary operations been forbidden, the market would have retained its imperial heights or declined so gently that all knowledgeable participants would have been warned and would have escaped. There was no mention of the hopes building on hope that had brought to so many the vision of great and enduring wealth, all pulling the market up, all subject to collapse when, on a day of anguish, something — no one would ever know quite what — fractured those fragile hopes, and the collapse led to yet further fracture and collapse. No one, the Marvins and their computer technician alone excepted, had seen the IRAT ratings.

By this misapprehension of the nature of the securities markets Marvin was not wholly distressed. As an economist, he sought public understanding. As a market operator making money, he knew it meant that the indices would again rise, euphoria would again return, the unique advantage of investing against putative insanity would still be there.

·   ·   ·

On the evening of the crash, as they went to bed, Marjie asked, "How should we feel about making so much money — money that so many others lost?"

"I can stand the pain," said Marvin. "Anyhow, we also did some good. We sold around the top, bought to cover our short position at the bottom. We were, don't you see, a stabilizing influence on the market."

"I see that, but I still wonder. So much sorrow; so many people took a bath. Why do they talk about taking a bath?"

"Removing the grime of unjustly accumulated wealth. Anyway, that sounds good. They should have remembered what Marx said: 'Where is the medal without the reverse?' "

"I'm glad to hear you quoting Marx," said Marjie. "It relieves my mind. You're not the quintessential American, your thoughts fixed only on making money."

"I'm not," Marvin assured her. "But I don't entirely regret getting rich."

"Let's go on now to the next stage," said Marjie. "Remember what we agreed: the money is just a means to an end — a greater end."

"I'm aboard," said Marvin. "But I also worry a little about our local situation. Our operation, as we call it, is pretty certain to be known now. You remember that professor out in Newton."

"You said that cutting Harvard in might be a good idea."

"Something we must now consider."

.　　.　　.

Harvard's need for help and the Marvins' response would come in the not too distant future. And one plea, at least, would come very soon. But first there was the matter of new living and office arrangements.

The well-worn Prescott Street apartment was no longer large enough. The twins and the fugitive daily help could use more space. More office workers and equipment would be needed for the activities they had in mind. Perhaps in pursuit of the public good there would have to be meetings. They looked at an exceedingly capacious ark on Brattle Street and decided that it would be ideal. They bought it for a little more than a million, now no longer an impressive sum.

Meanwhile, through the deeper interstices of the university community, in a process as osmotic as anything in nature, information was passing. Professor Marvin was said to have some kind of fix on the economic future. It had served him well in the recent stock market debacle; it had allowed him, it was said, to get out in time. No one quite knew what it was he had; more than any other subject matter, economics has its conceded mysteries. But now there was this new house; the Marvins' financial position had surely changed.

Proof came in varied forms and episodes. Once Marvin went into the Cambridge Trust on Harvard Square to cash a check. At the door he was overtaken by the dean, the genial, indifferently clothed but professionally perceptive man whom he and Marjie had visited that evening in Newton. The president of the bank came forward from his desk at the back of the large enclosure which he shared democratically with lesser officials, loan officers and secretaries. He shook hands warmly with Marvin, nodded courteously to the dean and then carried Marvin's check away to be cashed. The dean went into the line for the tellers. In such fashion, in the financial world and not less around a university, is information conveyed.

There was also general awareness of Marjie's continued activities on behalf of women, of which a word presently. These could not be carried out without expense.

It was this accumulation of knowledge about the Marvins that led to Professor Grierson's comment at the long table and to Joseph Craftwin's alert at the *Globe*. And from the latter came the pilgrimage by Eldon Carroll and the story back with the truss ads. If not yet in the league with Boone Pickens or Michael Milken, Marvin was no longer merely an astringently orthodox economics professor, the image that, more than he knew, he cherished.

.   .   .

Soon after moving to Brattle Street, the Marvins had a small housewarming and invited their neighbors and a few friends from Harvard. Such occasions, they were aware, do much to smooth and soften relationships. They act in a small way against the more acerbic tendencies of academic life.

The guests moving through the rooms of the old house were not entirely reassured. Well-used furniture, television sets, books and toys were all acceptable. However, there was also a glimpse through inadvertently opened doors of desks and desk chairs, telephones, green filing cabinets, stacks of paper, the computer bank, the printer. This was disturbing.

A lawyer of mature years who still served a few clients in his own adjacent domicile sought Marvin out. "It looks as though you might be doing some business here," he said, an inquiring note in his voice.

"Not really," said Marvin. "An economist's life is pretty complicated these days, and I'm involved in a few private matters as well."

"I'm glad to hear you say that's all. We like to think of this as a residential area. The real Cambridge, you know."

"I think you can count on me to respect your concerns," said Marvin.

"That's very, very reassuring," said his neighbor. "We're rightly careful about these things in this community." He paused for a moment and added a final thought for emphasis: "I helped lead the fight to keep the Kennedy Library out of here. That was a real achievement. It would have brought a lot of cars and questionable people into the neighborhood. And, anyway, the Kennedys didn't really come from here. Now the thing is over by the ocean, where it doesn't generate all that much traffic."

He moved away, and a familiar figure took his place.

"It was nice of you to come by, Professor Mc-Crimmon. You live near here, I believe?"

"Down Willard Street. A plebeian neighborhood. There is something I'd like to ask you. Just a thought or two I'd like to share. May we have a talk?"

Marvin took McCrimmon into his workroom. Mc-Crimmon sat in his desk chair; Marvin leaned back against a filing cabinet.

"You have heard of my old Scotch mentor, Herschel McLandress, I'm sure. Dr. McLandress."

Marvin was not sure, but he nodded as though in agreement. In university life one is always hearing mention of important names and books of which one does not know.

McCrimmon continued. "I picked up his work here at Harvard. The Psychometric Center. The McLandress idea was the codification of people according to the maximum span of time their minds could be diverted from themselves — millisecond men, five-second men, half-hour men. Women, too, of course."

It seemed vaguely familiar to Marvin, or so he thought. He nodded again.

"We run tests on prominent men and women which are based on secondary material. Ronald Reagan has a very high rating. His thoughts are on the country, the Nicaraguan contras and his old Hollywood days. Not on himself. Very good for a statesman."

"What about his Vice-President, Mr. Bush?"

"Less detached. A five-second man. Sometimes down to milliseconds. His thoughts are strictly on himself and his future."

"That's very revealing," said Marvin. "What about Mrs. Thatcher over in England?"

"Like Reagan. A very high rating. Her mind dwells on Britain and her husband, almost never on herself."

"Did you measure Henry Kissinger?"

"We did. Our work on him, though, is a bit out of date. But we do have some important local studies under way. Our researchers are now running tests on professors in the various graduate schools — business, law, arts and sciences, government, public health. Are there professionally correlated values? We're getting some very interesting results."

"Such as?" asked Marvin.

"Business and law. Very high factors of self-rejection. Surprising. Not what you would expect. Our Business

School people are now diverted from introspective personal concerns, inner-directed attention, by their fascination with business ethics. Similarly the lawyers. *Pro bono publico* work."

"I agree, that *is* surprising. Not at all what I'd heard elsewhere," said Marvin. "But what, more precisely, do you have in mind?"

"We wondered if you would like a consulting role at the center. Grierson says your index — IRAT, isn't it? — is based partly on psychometric measurements. I'm not playing any serious role myself, but I keep an eye out, try to lend a helping hand."

"That's very interesting," said Marvin.

"Let me come to the point. We'd like to tap you for some financial support."

"I'll certainly take it under advisement," said Marvin.

.   .   .

It was a foretaste of much to come. In the months ahead he and Marjie would take many requests under advisement. As they knew, not even the Ford Foundation or the MacArthur ever turned down out of hand an application for assistance; always it was taken under advisement.

Still, it was plain that out of their new wealth they would have to do something for Harvard. And unknown to them the great opportunity was coming. Meanwhile, though, there was a small enterprise of Marjie's to be furthered. And, of course, more money to be made.

· 10 ·

P P W

THE MONEY continued to roll in. The Bank of America, Marjie's first adventure, was a pleasant source of revenue. It had descended from its majestic position as the first bank of the country, a glowing example of agricultural, retail and real estate banking expertise, to near prostration, and its stock, to the Marvins' delight, reflected in dismal numbers the descent. The large Texas banks that Marvin and Marjie had visited when they were making their early assessment of euphoria were equally remunerative. The collapse of the RepublicBank Corporation, become the First RepublicBank Corporation, a holding company with forty banks scattered over the state, was worth some tens of millions of dollars alone. This might be small as compared with the truly lofty returns from the great stock market correction, but it was rewarding nonetheless.

Given the reliability of IRAT — the certainty when euphoria verged on insanity or the only slightly smaller certainty when pessimism built on despair — there had come to be an even more automatic aspect to the operation. Much could be given over to the computer and the discreet and adequately compensated young man who, increasingly, came to handle the routine. He, in turn, was now aided by two newly acquired assistants, one a highly efficient, wholly presentable young woman who had been superbly trained in computer science at both Haverford and Bryn Mawr. Marvin and Marjie knew they could no longer postpone serious pursuit of the liberal goals that until now had been only in the realm of intention and promise.

Their first effort was, however, suitably modest, a continuation of Marjie's earlier interest in the executive status of women. Perhaps it was less important for its eventual success than for bringing a new friend into their lives.

A few blocks from the Marvins' house, on Appleton Street, lived a woman of Marjie's age and of ancient New England lineage named Helen Winthrop Wentworth. Unattached after a brief and eminently instructive marriage, she had resumed her maiden name, moved back into her now deceased parents' house and, perhaps in reaction to the extravagant male chauvinism of her former spouse, had interested herself in a modest way in the women's movement. She had come to admire Bella Abzug, had read Betty Friedan and once had entertained Gloria Steinem overnight on a visit she was making to the Schlesinger Library on the History of Women in America at Radcliffe. Win, as she liked to be called, had a young son at school with the twins, and bringing the children home, she came to know the Marvins. Slender, attractively attired, at times what was once called demure, she was in sharp contrast with the increasingly robust

Marjie. This Marvin did not find unappealing; she, in turn, found more than acceptable any man who was as markedly different from her discarded husband as Marvin.

Marjie moved promptly to get Win interested in the Executive Gender Survey, and a new idea for increasing the number of women in the upper reaches of corporate management was discussed one lovely early summer evening on the terrace back of the Brattle Street house.

.   .   .

As food manufacturers were required to list the ingredients of the marmalades and cookies they sold and drug companies the chemicals in their medicines, so, in plausible continuity, corporations would be asked to list the percentage of women in their executive ranks. A tag or sticker on the product would convey this information, and female consumers, those now known to be largely in control of the expenditures from family budgets, would be asked to withhold patronage from any product without one. At Marjie's urging, the salary level above which this information would be required would be a modest $45,000.

"The pay must be within the range of middle-class aspiration. What I mean is that the average dame must see it as a real possibility for herself."

Companies employing fewer than five thousand people, they decided, would be exempt; the tag or sticker on their products could so state. As a further step, those with more than five thousand employees and publicly traded stock would be asked to provide similar information in their annual reports for the benefit of women investors.

Women, not men, were the ultimate beneficiaries of rather more than half of all the revenues from invested funds. The great New York investment houses would also be asked to provide the ratios of female to male executives in companies whose stock, bonds or junk bonds they were about to sell.

It was Marjie's idea that all this should be a matter of legislation. "The law says that we must be told the amount of fiber or mouse droppings in our bran flakes. Let us be told the number of women involved in running the companies that make the stuff. We have more than half the votes. Surely we can get the politicians to pay attention."

Marvin demurred. "It would be a hard struggle. I really don't think we have the leverage yet."

"Leverage is a Wall Street word. We're talking about the fair and decent treatment of human beings."

"I still think it would be too difficult."

Win came in with a word of agreement with Marvin. Her married years had been in Washington, and she had had, secondhand, some experience with the Congress.

Marjie relented. "Then let's try a volunteer effort. 'Women of the world, unite; demand the EXEGES sticker.' The new union label. Women do most of the shopping."

"I'll go along with that," said Marvin. "But I have some difficulty seeing Gloria Steinem in a supermarket with a shopping cart sorting through cans of asparagus looking for the sticker. Also, how does this work for steel, chemicals and the like? You don't go into a Stop and Shop, the Star or Bloomingdale's for those things."

Marjie responded, "You buy automobiles, and they're

made of steel. At least they used to be. And chemicals
go into garden fertilizer. And rubber into rubber tires.
We close down on the end products. That will somehow
get reflected back. To get this started, though, we'll need
some money for publicity."

"Money's certainly available," said Marvin, "but I
might keep myself a little in the background."

"That was to be expected," Marjie said pointedly but
with a pleasant tone in her voice. "How about you, Win?"

"Count me in."

The brakes on a car out on Brattle Street brought a
vehicle to a screeching halt. A pedestrian or maybe a dog.
The noise somehow sealed the agreement.

.   .   .

In large measure it came to seem Win's enterprise. The
Brattle Street house was now bursting at the seams, but
her house, which was of the same scale and vintage, had
a near infinity of extra space.

She and Marjie and two eager women graduate students
whom they hired set about compiling a list of the heads
of the two thousand largest American corporations, and
a letter on the impressive letterhead of The Executive
Gender Commission, listing the names of previously involved participants, was sent out to tell them what would
now be expected.

Word went also to Wall Street asking companies with
publicly traded securities to provide gender information
in annual reports and in connection with stock offerings;
the company executives were subtly reminded of the large
number of securities in women's hands. MMM, the advertising agency from which Marvin's father had now

retired, was brought on board to create ads for the women's magazines and to arrange radio and television spots. A public relations firm was recruited to get word into the press and on television talk shows. After a short waiting period while the manufacturers arranged compliance, shoppers would be asked to look for the tags. Any tagged merchandise should be considered better than untagged, and that with the best rating should be the one the shopper bought.

The effort caught on modestly well, the first effect being felt in the financial world. That was because a stock offering by Salomon Bros. that stressed the good gender record of the food company being financed was largely taken up by Marvin and went almost immediately to a premium. Its IRAT rating had been very low. The word on Wall Street was that the sex disclosure had done it. It is generally accepted that in the financial world information, both accurate and otherwise, moves, quite literally, with the speed of sound. Almost at once new offerings told of what came to be called the gender pattern.

Soon products with tags and stickers appeared in the stores. Some that showed a low percentage of women employed carried a neatly printed promise of improvement.

There were to be foreign repercussions. The Japanese, the most male-dominated of all the great industrial societies, faced the choice between tagless and stickerless merchandise, which might be downgraded and even rejected by the large American outlets, or tags bearing an abominable zero, indicating that no women were employed in executive positions. Reacting with characteristic acumen, Japanese businessmen discovered that the cost of adding a modest number of women at the minimum salary to improve the percentage in their ranks was less than the loss from their absence. Even if those thus recruited did not prove to be economically useful, their role, nonetheless, could be decorative and professionally affectionate. As so often before, the Land of the Rising Sun was now warmly praised for its accommodation to change. In later years the president of Mitsubishi was accorded a special citation by NOW, the National Organization for Women, and invited to address its annual convention. He was unable to accept. The greatest success, by a wide margin, would be in Japan.

All this was in the future. In the present, Marjie was dissatisfied. The response she thought too modest. The women's movement had lost its old dynamism, its old capacity for anger and insult. "Women are now too nice, too sedate. I liked the old days, when the bras got pitched into the garbage cans, chairmen became chairpersons, congressmen became congresspeople and we got indignant at places called Mannheim, Amman and Manhattan and thought well of Damascus."

She was addressing Marvin and Win. "Anyway, we didn't get rich in order to persuade people. We got rich in order to control people. The positive power of wealth. PPW. I'm going to have it sewn on my blouse over my right breast. Maybe put on an arm band."

She didn't. But in the coming weeks visitors to the house on Brattle Street saw the monogram PPW stitched in unduly pronounced black velvet ribbon on the white curtains in Marjie's downstairs study and office. Asked about it, she said it remembered a much loved aunt whom

she often went to visit as a child in Oakville, Ontario.
There had been horses to ride.

There was still much to do.

. . .

As EXEGES brought Win, her trim, charming presence
and her active, even eager mind solidly within the Marvins' life, it also brought her Washington experience. Her
former husband had been, still was, a partner in one of
the capital's largest and most distinguished law firms. His
pasture, like that of many of his partners, was Capitol
Hill; his assigned clients were the large canning companies — vegetables, fruits, meats and meat products — all
of them innately fearful of an extension of federal juris-
diction over the contents of their cans and not less over
their employees, including the farm workers whom some
hired and on whom all depended.

From her experience, magnified by both the congenital
meanness of her husband and the self-indulgent recital
of his successful assaults on the public interest, Win
had developed a decidedly adverse view of the influences
bearing on the national legislature. This had not been
improved by association with her husband's close professional friends from other distinguished law and consulting
firms who encouraged and guided the Pentagon and Congress on behalf of unequivocally lethal commerce. On all
these matters she was an informed voice, one that was
presently to be of much influence.

. . .

Outwardly, Marvin's life was quiet. His support of
EXEGES, though recognized, attracted little comment.

It was the sort of thing in which any professor with an energetic, determined wife might be involved. It was known that he had money; one used money for a good cause, as this surely was. Meanwhile his routine went on with only slight change. He taught his classes, went to his workshops and supervised a Ph.D. thesis or two, including a particularly subtle one by a young man from High Point, North Carolina, who sought to apply Marvin's own market theory and econometric methodology to the furniture industry amid which he had been reared. Harvard economics was pressing into a yet more applied phase.

Marvin was also conscious of the new respect, even measure of authority, he was now accorded in the community. When he walked down Brattle Street to the university of a morning, colleagues from the abutting streets now turned to await him or they overtook him on his way.

"How do you see the economic situation now, Marvin?"

"What do you think will be the legacy of Ronald Reagan?"

"I hear you're giving the women a hand on this new crusade of theirs. Very good, if I may say so."

Sometimes there were warnings: "Our friend Grierson tells me that you have a new forecasting wrinkle for telling what's going to happen to the economy. That must take a lot of your time. I hope you won't overdo it. Remember, your health comes first."

At economics department meetings, he was, on occasion, asked for his opinion. A new field of concentration to be approved, a younger colleague to be promoted.

Traditionally at Harvard opinions are offered; to be asked
was a rare and exceptional compliment.

Marvin, perhaps more than he knew, was becoming a
local figure, not a celebrity but in the academic reference
"something of a person." His next enterprise would further remove the wraps, and it would first come to light
at a faculty meeting he did not attend.

· 11 ·

THE RESCUE

HARVARD FACULTY MEETINGS are held once a month on Tuesday afternoons during the academic year, and except when issues of grave and potentially combative concern cause unusual attendance, as in the late 1960s, and a larger meeting room is required, the faculty members assemble on the second floor of University Hall. Tea or coffee, of which not all partake, is served at 3:30 P.M.; the meeting begins at 4:00 P.M. This is the Faculty of Arts and Sciences, which is looked upon, not least by itself, as the prime guiding authority of the university. The faculties of the Law School, Business School, Medical School, Schools of Education and Public Health, as also of the Kennedy School of Government, meet in separate conclaves, and of their proceedings very little is known.

On a surprisingly pleasant late March day — the New England climate is said to offer only one such day between the time when it is too wet and nasty and when it is too warm and uncomfortable — the president of the university, in keeping with established custom, strolled across from his offices in Massachusetts Hall, by a comfortable margin the most beautiful building in Harvard Yard — proving again the reliable diminution of architecture as an art — to the offices of the dean, which are adjacent to the large meeting room of the faculty over which he presides.

"We haven't much business again this week," said the dean after they exchanged greetings. "It's getting a bit troublesome. I wonder if we shouldn't propose another change in the curriculum. That's always good for a year or two. Maybe something like an inner core requirement?"

"No problem today," said the president. "Look at this."

It was a letter co-signed by the presidents of Morgan Guaranty, the Bank of Boston and, as an engaging local touch, the Harvard Square branch of BayBank, a short distance away from where they were sitting and once, no less, the Harvard Trust. It said that a client with a distinguished investment record and "a close association with Harvard" was offering to take over "all securities owned by the university that have been subject to criticism from various quarters because of the alleged participation of the designated corporations in the economic life of the Republic of South Africa." The offer would be at 10 percent over the closing prices on the New York Stock Exchange as of the previous Friday; its purpose was "to spare the university further possible embarrassment and adverse publicity in connection with these holdings."

"When did you learn about this?" asked the dean.

"Late yesterday afternoon. I intended to get in touch

with you. I've talked with the treasurer and the financial people over at Harvard Management. Also with all the members of the Corporation I could reach by phone." The Corporation, always mentioned at Harvard with some reverence, is the very small assemblage of distinguished and concerned men and in later times one woman that has charge of the practical, financial and, on occasion, sordid side of university affairs.

"What was the reaction?"

"Surprise. Even some awe. Naturally our financial friends don't like it thought they are making snap judgments. Or yielding to political concerns. In the end, however, even they were inclined to say we should accept. That 10 percent, after all."

"Who is this savior? What's his angle?" asked the dean.

"One of our own professors. He hasn't been officially identified. Completely reliable, they say. Anyway, the banks are involved."

"I could make a pretty good guess," said the dean. "It's that young professor in economics. He's said to have a system that's been making it big in the stock market."

"I can't say, but, unofficially, you're on the right track. Something like Data Resources. That was started by one of our professors. Eventually sold for millions."

"No, not like Data Resources. It sold financial and other advice. This man simply charts his own course, doesn't let others in on it."

"Very risky, I should think, but we do have the banks. Anyway, we have to keep his name off the record for the time being. That's a condition of the sale."

"What are you going to tell the faculty?"

"About the offer. I'll have to say it's from an affluent

friend of the university. He's bound to be known in a
few days. President Kennedy once said there were no
secrets in the United States government except a few
things he needed to know. Here there are no secrets at
all."

"It's time to go."

.   .   .

In earlier years divestment by Harvard of its South African–tarnished holdings had, indeed, been a matter of
lively contention. A white South African official, un-
wisely present in Cambridge, had been formidably pick-
eted, bringing a charge that serious principles of freedom
of speech were at risk. A wise and tolerant administration
had left undisturbed for some months the shanties that
appeared in the Yard next to University Hall. There were
continuous meetings and demonstrations that year and
protesting placards and arm bands at the commencement
exercises. Divestment had come up at faculty meetings,
to the pain of those who handled the university's finances,
none of whom felt that such issues should ever intrude
on calm, politically virginal financial action. Eventually
the agitation diminished and for a time disappeared.

All concerned with student behavior in American universities are poignantly aware of a basic tendency, one
that makes their administrative lives tolerable: students
involved in specific social issues — treatment of minor-
ities, ROTC, the environment — have an attention span
of around a year. Then the fashion changes, and so does
the issue. Only Vietnam was an exception, and that could
have been because of the threat of possible personal participation. Otherwise, if one has patience, all will pass.

Only rarely will some new act of outrage or oppression revive interest.

But that had now happened as regards South Africa. The South African government, ever more beset, ever more vulnerable to the siege and besieged mentality and reacting, as not rarely happens, against previous mild reforms, had in the preceding months extended its stern supervision to religion.

Black religious leaders — the Most Reverend Desmond Tutu, the South African Anglican Archbishop of Cape Town, possessor of an honorary degree from Harvard and a member of its slightly ceremonial Board of Overseers; the Reverend Allan Boesak, president of the World Alliance of Reformed Churches; other and lesser figures — had for years been, in apt metaphor, a heavy cross for the Pretoria government to carry. Churchly congregations, assembled for prayer and religious instruction in the black houses of worship, were thought to be dangerously available for political agitation. So it had been once in Montgomery, Alabama, in the time of Martin Luther King, Jr. The South African government was both adamant and increasingly logical. If God had intended whites and blacks to live together, they would have been living together in biblical times and before. The Last Supper would have been an integrated evening. At the distribution of the loaves and fishes there would have been a representative group of men and women of color. Apartheid was no matter of contemporary discovery and preference; a deeper theology was in control.

So the inevitable. Black churches, the places of contention, were closed or, more humanely, were turned into emergency nursing centers for those wounded in the ensuing protests. Church leaders were interned, some of them fleeing to Britain and the United States, where they had a generally warm reception. In Washington it was said that the new tragedy might have been avoided by a deeper and more consistently constructive engagement, but even there the adverse reaction was evident. Harvard did not escape.

On the contrary. Professors and students were actively united in opposition to the acts of the South African regime. The Divinity School faculty, which was often divided on matters of religious doctrine, now closed ranks and assumed leadership in support of the black community. The Harvard Law School Forum, traditionally and proudly known for giving voice to dissident and even insufferable views, met and reluctantly postponed an invitation to former President Botha, who was resting at White Sulphur Springs, West Virginia, after a visit of conciliation to the United States. Divestment was again, as it was said, very much on the university agenda.

. . .

The room into which the president and the dean now passed is, by common consent, the most attractive at Harvard. It extends the full width of the second floor of the rectangular, beautifully proportioned building. High windows on each side flood it with light. To the west they look down on the statue of John Harvard or, more precisely, of the handsome youth who in later years was persuaded to sit for the statue of the immortal benefactor, of whom no adequate description has survived. The faculty members occupy long rows of chairs on John Harvard's side of the room. On the opposite side, the view is of the Tercentenary Theatre (the lawn on which the commencement exercises are held), the imposing façade of Widener Library and the starkly white steeple of Memorial Church. Below the windows on that side of the room is a large round table. Here seated are the president, the dean and the secretary of the faculty. On the walls at each end of the room are the portraits of past presidents, deans, professors and other noted or diligent figures in the service of the university. The scholars of an earlier age are formidable; the more recent ones are approachable and in one or two cases even affable. In a corner of the room is a handsome grandfather's clock and on flagstaffs behind the president's chair a Stars and Stripes and another flag, which is of highly uncertain identity to many but is, in fact, that of Harvard.

On this day the Secretary's Report was quickly disposed of, and so also the Dean's Business, the president having announced that he would postpone his own business for later consideration. The gathering listened then with respectful attention to a Minute on the Life and Services of a well-loved professor of Byzantine history, dead these several years. It is one of the regrets of all at Harvard that these tributes, though literate, warm, sometimes affectionate in content, are often gravely delayed in preparation.

.   .   .

By the end of the reading, the last of the late arrivals had found their seats. Some further items on the docket having been disposed of, the president took the floor.

He said that he wanted to "advise the faculty of some news of which in the next days they would almost certainly be hearing more.

"In past years," he went on in a casual, mildly didactic

tone, "we have been cautious about responding to political and moral pressures where the university endowment is concerned."

At the back of the room a young professor in jeans, sweater and a shirt with an open collar said, "That's certainly true," but he was heard only by his immediate neighbors.

"We have not, however, been unaware of our responsibilities in this regard. We have had the Committee on Shareholder Responsibility designed to bring such pressure as may be possible on the corporations in which we have an interest."

"No results having yet been seen," said the man in the sweater.

"Now, I need hardly tell you, we see a new situation in South Africa."

"How perceptive!" This time it was a trifle louder. The professor in the next chair put a finger to his lips.

"I emphasize, we have a new situation, and we have also a new course of action. We are hoping to divest ourselves of the securities of companies that are actively engaged in South African operations."

A stir and a few whispers ran through the audience. Everyone was heard to shift position on the mildly uncomfortable chairs.

After a brief pause, the president continued: "It will not be at cost to the university. A friend, who for the moment wishes to remain unnamed, has offered to take all of our South African–related securities off our hands — out of our portfolio. This will be at prices substantially over those in the current market. Our financial people are still studying the offer, but they have already indicated that, after careful consideration, they will almost certainly accept. I, personally, have concluded that we *should* accept. A sizable sum is involved — around two hundred million dollars, as you may perhaps know. It relieves all of us, if I may say so, of a very controversial burden."

For a moment there was total silence. Then came an unmistakable murmur of approval.

After looking around to see if anyone else sought the floor, Professor Grierson rose to express his support. He did so at some length, citing the economic advantages inherent in what he referred to, perhaps unfortunately, as "this very good deal." Two other professors more briefly expressed their own satisfaction. The young man in the sweater and jeans was noticeably silent. Sensing the general mood, McCrimmon rose to speak. He had been sitting in his accustomed place at the far end of the front row of faculty seats. He was still clad in the heavy Harris tweed of winter. The president could not entirely avoid his eye.

"This is a matter of some importance," McCrimmon said, giving the impression that others disagreed, "and I wonder if we shouldn't have more extended debate. For one thing, shouldn't we know the name of this 'friend of the university'? It could affect our public position. I'm thinking of Donald Trump. Or that automobile man DeLorean. Maybe Michael Milken. I suppose it wouldn't be Ivan Boesky."

The president interrupted to assure McCrimmon, "It's not any of them."

McCrimmon continued: "I'm glad to hear that. But is anything gained by transferring these stocks and bonds to other ownership — less reasonable people, I would like to think, than ourselves? Aren't we just shedding a problem of our own and giving it to someone who doesn't have our sense of responsibility?"

Becoming aware that he still wasn't getting a sufficiently hostile reaction, he shifted ground once more. "In any case, there was surely something pretty predictable about this South African situation. The so-called Christians there practice apartheid in this world; isn't it reasonable for them to want it in the next? Does anyone suppose they want to go on to a fully integrated paradise? Blacks and coloreds on the golden streets? Shouldn't we leave them to practice their particular brand of Christianity in their own way? Our quarrel is only with the high logic of their action."

It was a long speech even for McCrimmon, and when it was over, there was another stir, this one of relief. The president, knowing from long experience that it was useless to respond, declared the meeting at an end.

.   .   .

The identity of Harvard's would-be rescuer was the dominating, indeed the only topic under discussion in the departing throng. Professor Grierson hazarded the guess that it might be a colleague of his. McCrimmon, who was close by and heard him, remembered his meetings with Marvin, the visit from the man at the *Globe* and other well-substantiated rumors and was not in doubt. Forgetting his own earlier questions, he now made known to all who were disposed to listen his firm view as to who had made this welcome offer, while expressing doubt as to whether it was a proper action for a member of the faculty.

Later that evening the dean discussed the matter in strict confidence with his wife and two other professors. Elsewhere the information spread. The *Crimson*, the most mature and skeptical of all college newspapers, first reported the divestment and then in the following issue said that the unknown benefactor was Professor Montgomery Marvin. The next day the *Globe*, as ever stirred to effort by Craftwin, had the same story, and *The New York Times* eventually ran several paragraphs about Marvin from its Boston bureau. Reporters from two local television stations descended on the Brattle Street house but were not admitted. A few days later Marvin observed an NBC team and the highly recognizable Tom Brokaw convening on the front lawn. He went out the back door and through a neighbor's yard to Win's. Marjie went too, leaving the young man who worked on the computer to answer the doorbell and explain that no one was at home.

Marvin continued to avoid press, radio and television, and very soon, in keeping with media tradition, interest almost completely subsided. However, the Marvins' anonymity, already impaired, was now at an end. With Marjie taking the lead in the months to come, they settled on a plan that would even more urgently engage the attention of Mr. Brokaw and his employers.

· · ·

A few days after the faculty meeting Marvin had an early morning phone call from the president of the university, asking if he could stop by on his way into the office from his house a few blocks farther out and just off Brattle. When he arrived, he told Marvin that, not surprisingly, his offer had been accepted and expressed the wish that more members of the faculty were similarly able to come to the support of the university. He hoped that this was the beginning of a mutually rewarding relationship. Harvard was blessed with many opportunities and had also many needs.

Marvin said that he would certainly take any such opportunities and needs under advisement.

. . .

That evening Marvin looked again at the computer printouts that calculated the IRAT for the Harvard investments. In the aftermath of the 1987 crash, there was still a small margin of reinforcing pessimism. He thought about whether he should share with the university the not insignificant profit that he would eventually realize from the sale of its erstwhile securities but decided that for the time being he would not do so.

· 12 ·

LET THERE BE

PEACE

P R I V A C Y, so ardently protected by law, custom and the many who wouldn't dream of suffering it, is a relative thing. The Marvins, in a certain if fragile sense, remained a private couple. They were thus described by friends and now repetitively by the press. They both, indeed, stayed much at home; their social life, as before, embraced only university colleagues, a few other local friends and Win. Their sex life was normal, thus uninteresting and, remarkably in this age, undiscussed. Neither their names nor their pictures had ever appeared in *People* magazine nor had those of the twins. They did not now.

With the Harvard endowment rescue and the attendant publicity, they had, however, become a private couple much in demand. Sought out in the Harvard and Cambridge communities, they also attracted invitations to social and money-raising events from the greatly distinguished in New York, Washington and, though more rarely, Los Angeles. People who had been introduced to them casually now spoke in intimate gatherings of an inseparable friendship; Marvin was quoted in the sort of detail that could only have surprised him. On his infrequent visits to the long table even the academically most urgent conversation stopped as attention turned to what he was saying. There was pressure to come to receptions to meet aspiring and sometimes deeply questionable politicians. All this, as best they could, the Marvins tolerated or resisted.

Marvin was also asked almost daily to give lectures and speeches. Occasionally, with some reluctance, he accepted. Thus one day, after especially vigorous persuasion, he crossed the Charles to lecture at the Harvard Business School to the Advanced Management Program — an assemblage of intelligent and talented men and women of early middle years, all confidently on the way to the top in their respective banks, investment houses and industrial corporations. He gave them a competent, devoutly technical and mathematical analysis of cyclical tendencies in refrigerator pricing and production, extending it, by inference, to certain other consumer durables. It was not understood. However, such was Marvin's reputation that his audience listened with every evidence of comprehension, and some described themselves afterward as inspired. Most lecture invitations he declined.

Increasingly, the Marvins were asked for money; their names, twice underlined and with stars, were now entered on all charitable and philanthropic solicitation lists. Particularly as a professor, Marvin was asked to help finance research and study on issues of public conscience and urgent social significance — housing and homelessness, drugs, teenage pregnancy, Zambian economic development, Polish enterprise zones and once a retrospective study of the psychiatric aspects of Department of Justice morale in the years of Edwin Meese. All such efforts were greatly in need of funds for staff and travel. For an hour or two each week the Marvins, sometimes joined by Win, leafed through the appeals and extended help to the seemingly most worthy causes. Their telephones, the numbers now unlisted, were kept connected to answering machines; one of their assistants listened at intervals to the tapes and told them of any messages that seemed to suggest relevance or compelling persuasion.

Their daughter continued to be subject to bouts of illness, and in the December following Harvard's Marvin-aided divestment she was taken to Children's Hospital in Boston with a badly inflamed throat that almost totally impaired her ability to swallow solid food. Word circulated that her condition was extremely serious, and a highly informal neighborhood committee was quietly set up to solicit memorial contributions from the Marvins and their friends for a community day care center on nearby Mount Auburn Street in the event that the child died. Promptness in such matters is known to be decisive; money must be obtained before grief or guilt is assuaged by time. Laura recovered.

Marvin and Marjie also contributed suitable amounts to the United Way and Marvin to his class gift to Harvard. On occasion, by form letter, they referred more formidable or questionable requests for support to research, study and travel to the Ford, Rockefeller, MacArthur or Annenberg Foundation or to the Carnegie Corporation.

Such now was the pressure on their well-known affluence that they rented several offices in a new and architecturally anonymous building down Massachusetts Avenue from Harvard Square toward Boston. This, their own house and Win's ample space on Appleton Street were all necessary to meet their expanding commitments.

Philanthropy and charity valuably express the determination of the rich to do good, while also giving them modest protection from the Internal Revenue Service. It was the Marvins' intention not to be confined to those causes which were so politically sterilized as to be tax deductible, for they, and especially Marjie, believed that concern over taxes effectively neutralized much otherwise worthwhile good-will expenditure. However, there are exceptions to all rules. Their next venture, modest in scale, was in the area of educational and thus tax-deductible effort.

·   ·   ·

The idea had emerged that day at Win's during the escape from the press. The conversation had turned, as so often before, to the continuing proliferation of nuclear weapons that is brought about by the obligatory commitment of all politicians to, as it is called, a strong defense. Why not, in the most decisive and formative places, have some countering movement — some education for peace? Make a start, a small start at least, toward ending the world's most suicidal obsession.

Marvin, still reflecting with slight unease on the money he was making on the sale of the securities from the Harvard divestment, was more than agreeable. Let there be a grant for education on and for peace. And let it be made to the most obvious recipients, the service academies — Annapolis and the Navy, West Point and the Army, and the Air Force Academy at Colorado Springs.

Marjie made the point. "They say they study war in order to win it and then have peace. Tell them to study peace in order to avoid war. Isn't that logical?"

"Very," said Marvin. "Do you think they will agree?"

"I once saw a television film on that secret base in Cheyenne Mountain out in Colorado," said Marjie. "It's where a lot of Canadian officers go. NORAD. The Air Force signs there say PEACE IS OUR PROFESSION. Let them prove it."

. . .

A few days later, after further discussion, Marvin drafted letters to the commandants of each of the three service academies. Each was offered an endowment to establish a chair "with research support" in peace studies. Teaching emphasis would be on negotiation instead of conflict, on arms control as an alternative to the arms race, on the means by which the war machine could most painlessly be dismantled and those engaged in such pursuits returned to peaceful employments. Win edited the drafts; Marjie offered suggestions for sharpening the tone. Marvin took the letters around to a neighbor who presided over Harvard's distinguished Program on Negotiation, a small group of scholars committed to conflict resolution without war. From them came further suggestions and strong approval. The letters were dispatched. To add a sense of urgency, they went by Federal Express.

The response of the academies did not come quickly. Clearly it was a matter requiring serious discussion and at a fairly high level, not excluding some reference to the

Joint Chiefs and the Secretary of Defense himself. Favoring acceptance were the ample grants that had been proposed, each $2.5 million, which would provide stipends well above the service pay levels to which teachers on assignment to the academies are held. What seemed to cause the greatest concern was whether this might make peace as a concept unduly prominent in the academies' routine. And also the names of the chairs as specified by the Marvins and Win.

There was no great problem at Annapolis; the Gene R. LaRocque Chair honored a distinguished admiral, one of the Navy's own. After retiring, Admiral LaRocque had dedicated himself and his organization, the Center for Defense Information, to the pursuit of peace, with special attention to the more egregious aberrations in Pentagon weapons procurement and planning. But he was, after all, a retired admiral; the Navy and Annapolis could not react against him.

The Army had only mild reservations about a William Sloane Coffin Chair, and it too yielded after a few weeks to the generosity of the grant. There was, however, considerably more uneasiness at Colorado Springs. Marjie and Win had wanted one of the chairs named for a woman. Their first thought was of Jeannette Rankin, the congresswoman from Montana who had voted against American participation in both world wars — the sole negative vote in the case of World War II. Her name, however, was unacceptable to some historically minded members of the Air Force faculty. There was also fear in larger military circles of a hostile congressional reaction. Time had made opposition to American participation in World War I eminently respectable. Not so that to the later and greater conflict with Hitler.

The Air Force objections, conveyed tactfully to the Marvins, were heard and accepted. A Caldicott professorship, named for the highly motivated Australian peace advocate, was considered instead, but, in the end, Marjie and Win surrendered. It would be the Bertrand Russell Chair. The Academy was delighted to honor a distinguished philosopher from another NATO country. The more insensitive of Russell's actions on behalf of peace and against nuclear arms and his extended prison confinement during World War I were no longer remembered. Nor by many in Colorado Springs was Bertrand Russell himself.

When the professorships were publicly announced, the reception accorded them was favorable. The Marvins received the applause of SANE/FREEZE, the Council for a Livable World, the Union of Concerned Scientists and the American Committee on U.S.-Soviet Relations. The press generally approved. Joseph Craftwin, now fully abreast of the Marvins' activities in Cambridge, commissioned an adulatory news story. A *New York Times* editorial, exploring both the pros and cons of the gifts, was thought by many readers to be, on balance, favorable. Several congressmen and senators expressed themselves, if cautiously, in support of the professorships, and Massachusetts legislators rallied rather strongly to their increasingly well known constituents.

Predictably, however, there was critical congressional reaction. It was said, without originality, that the professorships were a design for making the academies and their graduates soft on defense. A deeply concerned senator speaking that autumn to the annual convention of the American Legion went even further. "This," he avowed, "is a questionable effort to subvert the officer class of our United States and to insert subversive Communist propaganda into three of our most patriotic and otherwise sacred institutions. Are we, I ask, to have officers in our military who want peace and are against war? Are we to have men and some women leading our armed forces who are taught that they need not fight and die for their country, as you, my comrades-in-arms, once fought and died?" It was noted that the applause after his speech was surprisingly muted; those who had themselves experienced war were not uniformly impressed.

Even this limited condemnation abated, however, when the appointments to the chairs became known. In accordance with the accepted principles of academic freedom and the terms of the grants, these were made by the academies' own governing authorities. Selected to be the first William Sloane Coffin Professor at West Point was the distinguished Mr. Richard Perle, long an assistant to the late Senator Henry (Scoop) Jackson and latterly Assistant Secretary of Defense, who was now, with greater age, mature, mellow and many thought even reflective in his foreign policy positions. His appointment did much to counter the opposition. Those chosen to occupy the other two chairs were arms control authorities, one with particular credentials on the deeper theory of nuclear deterrence. They were uncontroversial.

.   .   .

The generally amiable reaction to the peace professorships did not prepare the Marvins for the minor commotion occasioned a few weeks later in Cambridge by the rumor that Marvin was endowing a chair at Harvard to honor

Professor Angus Maxwell McCrimmon. Rumors, someone once said, are the intellectual staff of academic life.

It was never clear whence the McCrimmon rumor
came, but it gained a measure of plausibility from the
Marvins' grants to the service academies and was
promptly accepted as fact. Those at the long table made
it a topic for atypically agitated conversation on the days
McCrimmon was absent. It also brought another meeting
between president and dean.

"This is going to cause real trouble," said the president.
"If it comes through, we can't turn it down. I hate to
think of the faculty reaction."

"McCrimmon will support it."

"But it will be a problem for him; he's never been with
the administration before."

"Why not give the chair to McCrimmon himself? Concentrate it all in one place. McCrimmon, the Mc-
Crimmon Professor."

"Yes, that he would accept."

The professorship did not materialize. There was eventually some thought that the rumor had been started by
McCrimmon himself.

As all this was happening, another matter abruptly demanded the Marvins' attention. It had its origin in a lin-
gering suspicion that, to the distaste and even despair of
all conservatives, continues to haunt the free enterprise
system. It is the feeling that no one can get very rich in
a very short time without crossing the ill-guarded border
into chicane or outright crookedness. The spirit of Jay
Gould, Daniel Drew or Gentleman Jim Fisk has never
been fully exorcised from the American memory.

Although plans were now under way for their next

project, Marvin found himself diverted by the ever vig-
ilant government of the United States.

. . .

For some time a new and at first puzzling circumstance
had come to mark his securities transactions. Always with
IRAT, although there was the agreeable certainty as to
the eventual movement up or down of the stock in question, there was some uncertainty as to when this would
occur. A high IRAT rating meant an earlier fall in price
than did a lower one, but it didn't inform as to precisely
when. So, vice versa, with a low or negative rating. But
now when Marvin sold or bought, the fall or increase in
the price was coming much faster. Clearly some clan-
destinely informed operators were following his trades.
The highly rewarding character of his sales and purchases
had been observed, and those so advised were acting on
their own behalf. One, perhaps several, of the brokerage
houses in Boston and New York over which, as a sensible
precaution, he was now distributing his business were at
fault, but he had no way of knowing which. He did not
greatly regret this piggybacking, as he knew it was called
in other circumstances. In theory, others were sharing his
monopoly of the information from IRAT; in practice,
their sales both hastened and, had that been necessary,
assured his own success. This allowed a faster turnover
of his now ample capital, an increase in his now flush
flow of return — a flow passing through the largest of
Boston and New York banks that was, as before, further
amplified by the credit being ever more eagerly supplied
to his operations.

There was, however, an unforeseen consequence. It
manifested itself one rainy Tuesday morning in Novem-

ber when, free of classes, Marvin was himself giving a hand on IRAT calculations in the computer room of the Brattle Street house. An answering machine took a call from the Securities and Exchange Commission saying that a couple of its representatives would like to pay him a visit the following morning. It was hoped that he would be present. This he was asked to confirm.

The next day two young men of surprisingly similar dress and appearance presented themselves at the door. Lean of face, clean-shaven, they wore London Fog raincoats, which, when removed, revealed brown worsted suits of somber and conventional cut. They showed Marvin their credentials, and he took the men into the living room, where, clearing away some toys and partly completed puzzles belonging to the twins, he invited them to sit down. This they did with no evident tendency to relax. Marvin now saw that one was slightly older and, if possible, of marginally more serious mien.

"We are from the SEC," the older man said somewhat unnecessarily.

"So I gathered," said Marvin. "What can I do for you?"

"I want to make clear," said the older man, who from the identification Marvin had seen had the musically evocative name of George Mozart, "that our presence here doesn't imply any felonious behavior on your part. We simply wish to discuss with you certain things that have emerged from a routine computerized survey of your investment operations."

It was a speech he had evidently made before.

"In accordance with our rules," he continued, "I'm obliged to tell you that we are both lawyers and to ask if you would like to have counsel present."

"I can't see why."

"Then we can proceed. With your permission we would like to have a record of our conversation. You are at liberty to make one too."

Marvin nodded his agreement and said he saw no need for one himself. The younger man took from his pocket a small Japanese tape recorder and tested it by counting to ten. After holding it for a moment to his ear, he placed it on a chair, which he pulled up before him.

"Why don't you take over, Al? This is Mr. Hague, Professor Marvin. Alois Hague."

"Thank you, George. Professor Marvin, this won't take too long, I hope. Our professional staff has been examining your market activities. That's routine for all nonroutine operations that come up on the computer. You seem to have an exceptional tendency to anticipate the market. In fact, our people haven't been able to come up with any exception. Are you aware of this?"

"Certainly," said Marvin. "Were there exceptions, as you say, I would lose money."

"You understand what aroused our interest?"

"I'm afraid not. I don't suppose you would want me — my wife and me, really — to lose money?"

"It's somewhat normal, Professor Marvin. You know what a record like yours signifies?"

"I don't believe I do."

Mr. Hague's voice took on an ominous, slightly threatening tone. "Inside information. Insider trading. That's what it signifies."

"You mean advance knowledge of mergers, leveraged buyouts, things like that? Boesky? Levine?"

"Precisely."

"But that anticipates rising prices. Heavy bids for the stock. Your people must have seen that we've been mostly on the down side. It's undue optimism, euphoria really, that we're programmed to identify. Is there anything wrong with that?"

"That we recognize to be a problem," said Hague. "But we also feel that there's something odd about your being so much on the negative side. Americans are meant to be optimistic. This country is built on optimism, you might say. Why this consistently negative" — he reached for the word — "this consistently negative attack on optimism, we might call it?"

"Markets do go down," said Marvin. "You wouldn't want everyone to be on the same side, would you?"

"We recognize that to be a problem. But let me proceed to another matter." He consulted some notes that he had brought out on his lap. "You were definitely long after the 1987 crash. Also after that Harvard buyout, if I may call it that."

"But the securities of dozens of companies were involved in both cases. I could hardly have had inside information on all of them. And they certainly weren't all involved in mergers or acquisitions, leveraged buyouts, junk bond operations."

"We recognize that to be a problem," said Hague.

George Mozart intervened. "That we recognize to be a problem. But your record gives us serious grounds for concern. People don't make money all the time; there simply have to be gains and losses. What is your explanation?"

"Come with me," said Marvin.

They went into the computer room. Marvin pointed to several bales of printouts and to the machines themselves and launched into his account. Going back to John Law and William Paterson, coming down to Freud, Jung

and Ivar Kreuger, to Bernard Cornfeld and on to Equity
Funding in Los Angeles and the seemingly explosive recent success of Drexel Burnham Lambert, and drawing
on some mathematical parallels from the refrigerator industry, he gave his visitors a brief technical overview of
the historical, philosophical, psychological and mathematical bases of the IRAT conceptualization. He added
that, while he had never publicized his method, any time
they wanted to come back, he would go into it in detail.

Mr. Mozart noted again that he and his colleagues were
lawyers. It would be for others to go into the technical
details; that would be *their* problem. "It would then be
our problem — Al here and myself — to judge whether
there had been any violation of the trading regulations.

"But let me now raise a further and final matter. It
appears from our surveillance that a certain number of
other people are following your trades. That suggests that
they have inside information on your purchases and sales.
Can you account for that?"

"I'm sorry to say I can't," said Marvin. "I like to think
that the brokerage houses with which I deal have the
highest of ethical standards. But there could be lapses."

"You agree that someone is operating on *inside* information on your trading?"

Marvin nodded assent.

After shaking hands, the two men left. Confident that
he was within the law, Marvin watched them walk down
the path to their car. He had the feeling that he might see
them again.

· · ·

As they drove off, George Mozart looked reflectively at
Alois Hague. "I think, Al, we have established pretty

clearly that there has been insider trading based on inside information on this man's trading. Not a level playing field."

"You mean insider trading based on noninsider trading?"

"Yes. Exactly."

"Doesn't that pose a problem?"

"Yes, a problem."

· 13 ·

THE PRCS

WIN HAD CONTINUED to nurse in something close
to clinical aversion the memory of marriage and her former spouse. Then one exceptionally lovely spring day
the newsboy left her by mistake not *The New York Times*
but *The Wall Street Journal*. To the right on the front page
was a more than adequately comprehensive article that
told of a spectacularly successful assault in the Congress
on the refined urban attitudes that had demanded toilet
facilities for berry pickers and lettuce hands. A companion
editorial many pages inside dealt with the same subject;
it called attention to the spacious natural equivalent on
every farm of a hundred septic-tank leaching fields and
praised the congressional resistance to toilets, saying they
were an egregious assault on free enterprise.

That Win's emotional reaction reached turbulent levels
was not wholly surprising. The chorus of congressional
indignation that had side-tracked the proposed regulation
was, she knew, the work of a Political Action Committee

guided by her former husband. This the *Journal* had affirmed, along with the fact that it was he who had drafted the most stirring of all the speeches on the subject, one that had been given by a masterful orator from California's Central Valley, who had begun by asking, "Who in this freedom-loving land is going to interfere with the basic right of every American, foreign or domestic, to relieve himself, as he needs and where he wills, on the open ground?"

Then, in keeping with the times, he had resorted to biblical support: "I ask you, my friends and colleagues, did Moses pass by motels on the way up the Mount? Did Saul seek out service stations on the road to Damascus?"

Win took the newspaper over to the Marvins', and Marjie was for action. Everything was going almost too well. The peace professorships had, on balance, been applauded. So also the Executive Gender tags, admitting always their rather small effect. And so, locally and gratefully, the Harvard bailout. The larger future beckoned.

"Why can't we have a Political Action Committee on the other side?" asked Marjie. "Political support for toilets. A demand for more Johnnies-on-the-Spot."

Marvin, his attention distracted for the moment from the day's instructions flowing from IRAT, agreed. After some further discussion, he put in a telephone call to Washington to Philip Stern, the acknowledged authority on Political Action Committees. Perhaps the Marvins should make the PACs the object of their next crusade. Stern was enthusiastic and promised all the guidance that his somewhat uncertain state of health would allow.

The basic idea emerged. For every contribution to a Political Action Committee let there be, somehow, a

countering contribution on the other side. Money off-
setting money. The principle was clear; only the details
needed to be worked out.

.   .   .

Unlike the peace professorships or, in the end, the Harvard rescue, this effort would not be inexpensive. But
cost was now only a minor factor. Euphoria and pessimism still alternated on the markets, and IRAT was as
effective as ever in isolating the excesses of each. The
scale of Marvin's operations had continued to grow; no
one experienced in these matters would ever doubt the
lush rewards from always being right. And here was a
chance to bring directly to bear the positive power of
wealth. Win, restrained but thinking angrily of her former
spouse, tied a small bouquet of daffodils to one of the
curtains in Marjie's office that bore the initials PPW. As
befits this world not of words but of acronyms and ab-
breviations, these three letters now had a secure place in
the Marvins' system.

.   .   .

From the excellent Mr. Stern came a list of all the Political
Action Committees currently representing corporate or
other obtrusive economic purpose — the National Rifle
Association, the United Parcel Service of America, Inc.,
Philip Morris, General Electric, the Northrop Corporation, Boeing, Grumman, Winn-Dixie Stores, Inc., the
canners who had so powerfully and adroitly reacted to
the toilets, some hundreds more. Excluded only were
those which spoke for the broader public interest. From
the comprehensive statistics of the Federal Election Com-

mission Stern had compiled figures on the flow of funds to individual senators and congressmen from the former organizations. A countering flow, dollar for dollar, would now go in opposition. Surely no legal obstacle could stand in the way of so virtuous a purpose. That was soon to be ascertained.

. . .

For well on to a century the intellectually most secure, even self-approving segment of Harvard University had been its greatly distinguished Law School. The law was there regarded as the sacred frame for man's well-being. Those who taught the subject spoke with reverence of its great scholars — Holmes, Pound, Frankfurter — and in only modestly more restrained terms of themselves. But in recent years this deep and serene conception had been assailed. A younger generation calling itself the Critical Legal Studies community had been led to ask if the law, so perceived and so revered, might not be the guardian and protector of privilege — of those whose power or pecuniary interest was favored by precedents and theses and by laws and legal decisions. Of this movement and its members the Marvins naturally were aware; Marvin, in his increasing loss of anonymity, was also well known to them.

One morning a few days after the discussion on Brattle Street and the talk with Stern, Marvin, Marjie and Win made their way under the stately trees of the Harvard North Yard, all in their disciplined columns, to Griswold Hall, one of the newer Law School structures, advertising in its internal aspect of gloom the extreme gravity of the subject. The question they sought to have answered:

How, money not being a restraining influence, could the power of the Political Action Committees — the PACs — be countered, not excluding the PAC so well served by Win's ex-husband?

The young lawyers who had assembled at Marvin's request did not conceal their enthusiasm for their task or seek, in the time-honored tradition of their craft, for possible complications that would show the depth of their legal acuity. Marvin's relief of Harvard from its South African embarrassment had given them a more than adequate impression of his financial resources, and this, in suitably general terms, he now affirmed. In the small seminar room in which they met, there was an air of only slightly suppressed excitement as Marvin outlined the problem he wanted solved. A young professor clad in a reputable blue blazer and grey trousers then took the floor; he tended a trifle to classroom rhetoric.

"The law is regularly stretched for questionable purposes. It is in the best spirit of our profession that this should now be done for a worthy cause. I think the needed design is rather simple. For the considerable scale of Professor Marvin's financial operations he obviously needs advisers, so bring corporations into being that are dedicated to giving that advice. He pays them for the advice, and out of these payments each corporation hires officers and a staff. These receive a modest compensation for themselves and generously contribute the rest to a form of Political Action Committee consisting of these same officers and employees. Let any contribution by a corporate PAC to a congressman or senator then be matched by a similar contribution from the committees formed by Professor Marvin's corporate advisers to whoever runs against him or her in the next election. Let this be strictly nonpartisan. And let each of the committees keep its individual contributions rigorously within the allowed limits."

He stopped for breath and to sense the reaction of his colleagues. This was evident in the nods of approval. A legal *tour de force*. Marvin alone seemed doubtful.

"I would be paying for something I don't need. IRAT — that's my forecasting formula, the Index of Irrational Expectations — gives me all the guidance I can use."

"Irrelevant," said the man in the blue blazer. "Anyone engaged in financial operations is expected to seek advice. Much of it, in the nature of the case, is worthless. The law in its admitted majesty cannot possibly distinguish between good financial advice and worthless financial advice."

"As you describe it, my advisers would be getting very little money for this advice, so called, and all the rest would go to the committee set up for political action. Won't that look pretty odd?"

"Very odd. But it can be defended as being for a splendid purpose. That's how the law should serve. And lawyers too. Let both embrace to the limit the public purpose. Anyhow, there is precedent. Corporations are known to be generous in their pay in order to cover PAC contributions."

A young woman, blond and intense, clad in only slightly faded jeans and a dark sweater, now intervened. "Do you really have lots of money?"

Marvin nodded. "Let's say that that is not a limitation."

"Then why not also a supplementary payment? Special

honoraria for anyone running against the PACs. Make the payments available through the local high schools and colleges. In the political world honoraria are now a lush source of money; they should be matched too. There would be an understanding that the candidate, if elected, would oppose all PAC–supported votes. That would also be at the highest ethical level."

There was further discussion, but the outlines of the enterprise were now clear. If a legislator took money from a Political Action Committee, his or her opponent in the next election would get the same amount, maybe even a little more, from a committee supported by Marvin's financial enterprises. Taking PAC money, a member of Congress would thus subsidize his or her own opposition; in a sense, corporate PAC money would pay for an opposing stand. Maybe then the congressman or senator would have second thoughts about PACs, and that would lead to a cut in the matching cost.

As the discussion ended, Marvin's mind went back to that evening in the other Cambridge. It had been pointed out then that liberals traditionally deplore the use of money for purposes adverse to the public good, and here in perfectly realized form was the solution offered in that distant living room. A liberal would get the money and then beat the moneyed interests with their own weapon.

Marvin was brought back to the gloomy classroom by a final question. "Don't you need a name?"

It couldn't, someone said, be another Political Action Committee — or committees. That had an evil connotation. It was Marjie who came up with the compelling suggestion.

"Why not the Political Rectitude and Integrity Committees? PRICs, for short." She pronounced the acronym with evident pleasure.

The woman in the slightly faded jeans demurred. "It sounds sexist to me."

One of the young male professors came forward with a compromise.

"Leave out the word 'Integrity'; it's redundant, anyhow. Call them the PRCs. That's perfectly innocent, and people will still refer to them as the PRICs if they wish."

It was agreed, and indeed as the PRICs in all spoken language they came to be known. The American idiom is not ill disposed to the mildly scatological.

Marvin invited all who were free to join him for lunch at the Faculty Club. As was usually now the case, there was a respectful show of attention, some nudging of visiting scholars into recognition, as Marvin led the party through the big room by the long table to the smaller dining room beyond. There would have been more nudging had the work of that morning been known.

.   .   .

In ensuing weeks the Marvins rented additional space down Massachusetts Avenue. The newly created corporations, which were scattered around the Boston area, needed directors, executives and nominal staffs, and these were recruited from the local community — young instructors, some sympathetic faculty members, motivated older and senior citizens, a minister or two, several liberal lawyers, one or two politicians. The equivalent of a daily messenger service was established to and from Wilmington, Delaware, where the exfoliated advisory firms were given their corporate home. It was never specified that any particular share of the money earned by the officers and employees of the advisory services would go to the corporate PRC; some things were to be understood. That they were compensated in a manner and amount that allowed of contributions to the PRC was a proposition for which there was, as noted, ample precedent from the corporate PACs. The PRCs merely carried this a step, perhaps several steps, further by making the personal reward nominal, the political payment decisive. It was, in the end, a surprisingly simple design.

It did nothing, nonetheless, to diminish the Marvins' visibility. Craftwin at the *Globe* called Eldon Carroll in once more. "There's something going on again over in Cambridge. Maybe you'd better just stay out there. Big money coming from that fellow Marvin's forecasting operation that you couldn't understand a few years ago. More than from old Joe Kennedy in his heyday, I hear, and going heavily into politics. Get over and see if you can do better this time."

Marvin was not available; at home he was thought to be at the university — he had spoken of the need to begin work on a paper for the next meeting of the American Economic Association which would extend to air conditioning some of his past thinking on the theory of refrigerator pricing. But he was not there or at Mass. Avenue, where three other reporters sat in his outer office against his possible return. At the Brattle Street house there were only the answering machines. Eventually Carroll was told that Professor Marvin was in the library and unavailable; he would, however, have a press conference in a day or two at which the PRC program would be fully explained.

Eldon Carroll called again on Professor McCrimmon, who said he had some information. He had heard rumors.

"A plan from Marvin's wife for more public toilets in our cities. People shouldn't be required to sneak into a hotel or find a service station. Like Paris and the *pissoirs* in the old days. A very sensible idea."

Craftwin told Carroll he had probably better wait for the press conference.

.   .   .

Marvin met the reporters with Marjie, Win and the lawyer in the blue blazer all present. It was in the small conference room at the Mass. Avenue offices. Initially much of the space was taken up by two television crews, who, however, turned off the lights and left when Marvin got down to the serious explanation.

It was brief. Marvin's financial operations on their present scale required expert outside advice, and a network of small independent corporations was being created to provide it. Asked about the possibility that they would be involved in political activities, Marvin said these would be allowed, even encouraged. "I think business enterprises should show an active interest in the public welfare."

He went on to observe that Political Action Committees were an established feature of American public life. No one doubted their purpose: it was to buy legislative support. His advisory enterprises would be urged to form what he had suggested be called Political Rectitude Committees, and any aspiring legislator who received contributions from them would probably vote in opposition to the PACs. But no promises would be exacted; it was in the American tradition that you didn't buy votes. You raised money for statesmen in whose intentions you had full trust.

The questions were prompt and to the point.

"Where is the money coming from?"

"From the PRCs of the companies that are giving me financial advice." He allowed himself the soon-to-be-accepted pronunciation — PRICs.

"You pay for that advice?"

"That's normal in the financial world."

"So the money comes ultimately from you?"

"Yes."

"How do you know if the advice you'll be getting will be any good?"

"I'll use only that which accords closely with my own considered judgment."

The reporters nodded and scratched busily on their pads. An obviously sensible answer.

There were further questions as to how much his affiliated corporations might commit to the PRCs. This Marvin declined to guess. "It would depend on how many would-be congressmen and senators take the pledge against the PACs in the election next autumn and thereafter." The word "pledge" went unnoticed except by the lawyer in the blue jacket.

In *The New York Times, The Washington Post* and across the country the birth of the PRCs was heralded in a modest way. And there was brief mention on television.

Rather more attention was given to this historic development in the House and Senate. There was general and at times intense discussion in the Capitol corridors and down in the restaurants. Staff members were assigned to do research and write reports on the new committees, and these told of an untoward, even dangerous threat, which, however, had to be treated with discretion.

Without quite knowing it, Marvin and Marjie had crossed the great divide, that which separates benign and agreeable liberalism, of which all politicians are known to be tolerant, from action, which often means serious and highly unwelcome trouble. Of this there would now be some indication.

· 14 ·

THE HEARING

FOR THE AVERAGE STATESMAN the Marvins' newest initiative did present an unpleasant choice. Either sacrifice an admirable flow of income from the PACs for electoral and ultimately perhaps more personal purpose or, by taking it, subsidize a competitor in equal amount from the PRCs. And there was a similarly nasty choice for each PAC itself: to continue the subsidy to a congressman was to help support the campaign of an opponent pledged — that forbidden word — to vote in opposition once in office. Needed restraints on inconvenient imports, the beleaguered tobacco manufacturers, undesired taxes and greatly desired tax loopholes were all at risk. Toilets would deface the pastoral fringe of the pristine California and Texas fields.

Yet there was an equitable quality about the whole development that called for a cautious response. To pay for opposition to legislation was not ostensibly more depraved than to pay for the legislation itself. The PRCs should, obviously, be opposed, but it was an operation to be undertaken with delicacy, and delicacy of action is not a natural attribute of democracy nor is it descriptive of the everyday procedures of the Congress of the United States. Still, something had to be done.

An informal bipartisan meeting of the more reliably discreet members of the House of Representatives assembled in the impressively squalid Capitol office of the Speaker, which had been borrowed for the occasion. After discussion, it was decided that the principle underlying the PRCs could not itself be attacked. Or the network of advisory corporations that "that fellow up there" had established. Corporate law under the free enterprise system is a thing of nearly unlimited flexibility; it allows always for a maximum accommodation of corporate structure to need. The legislators knew, since they were lawyers nearly all, that any effort against Marvin's complex of advisory corporations would only end, after a near infinity of time, in virtually incomprehensible legal justifications for inaction.

A plain-spoken plainsman from Oklahoma came finally to the point: "The real question is where this young bastard is getting that money. Where I come from, we happen to know that if something's really big, it isn't going to be honest. Let's get on to that."

It was decided eventually and accordingly to send a highly informal request to the SEC, asking it to have a look at Marvin's securities operations — the evident source of the largest part of his income. And it was further decided to have him called for examination by the House Banking, Finance, and Urban Affairs Committee, of which a cooperative and influential member happened to be on hand. It was in the public interest to identify what could, quite possibly, be ill-gotten gains. Thereby the public interest and that of the members of Congress would both be served.

A few days afterward discreet word came back from the SEC that, in accordance with its characteristic vigilance, Marvin's operations were already under surveillance. The tendency in the market for any security to go up or down in a relentlessly beneficial way to Marvin following his purchases or sales had for some time been evident from the computer tracking. And Marvin himself had been questioned. Lacking only was "sufficient" evidence of illegality; finding this had, it was said, posed a problem and would require more time.

The congressional hearing was scheduled, and Marvin was asked to appear. He got the invitation, which came by registered mail, one morning at breakfast. "Given the continuing concern of the Committee for the integrity and stability of our financial institutions, your rather sizable securities operations have been brought to the Committee's attention. It would be greatly appreciated if you would meet with the Committee." A date was proposed; the staff director would be in touch as to further details. There was no threat of compulsion.

·   ·   ·

The modern university professor whose field of expertise is economic policy, foreign policy, education, AIDS or drug abuse has an admirable experience with congressional hearings. In the absence of any other plausible or politically agreeable course of action in the American democracy, a committee hearing is called. Then, in the absence of any more obvious source of information, a professor is invited to testify. Members of no other occupation have such catholicity of knowledge so readily available.

This, somewhat exceptionally, was Marvin's first such appearance. No recent national emergency had centered on problems arising from the economics of refrigeration. Marvin read the letter of invitation with some concern; distant images of John Dean and John Ehrlichman and more recently of Colonel North and Admiral Poindexter passed disturbingly before his eyes. He made his way to Littauer Center and up the stairs to the second-floor corner office of Professor Grierson; it was down the hall from his own less spacious and now less frequented office, where his by no means overburdened secretary handled his routine academic affairs. Harvard has one-window professors and more privileged two-window professors; Marvin was one of the former, Grierson one of the more favored.

Professor Grierson's desk was under a pile of scholarly papers and monographs which there could be no plausible reason to believe he would ever read. He was the veteran, all knew, of many congressional hearings and of not fewer than twenty indecisive sessions before the Joint Economic Committee of the Congress, a committee that unites the best economic intelligence of the House of Representatives and the Senate. Marvin told him of being summoned. Evidently his market predictions and their use were to come under scrutiny, and he needed advice as to the proper course of action and behavior. Professor Grierson gave close attention to his query and his expression of concern and told him to relax.

"It's easy. When you know the answer to a question and want to give it, take lots of time, reply at real length. If you don't know the answer or don't want to respond, compliment the committee member warmly on the relevance of what's been asked and say it's something to which you will have to give further thought. You can't go wrong."

"What about unfriendly questions? You've heard of my Political Rectitude Committees. They probably aren't popular down there. In fact, I've heard word to that effect."

"I couldn't advise you on that. I've never had any hostile questions myself. You have a different situation, I would judge."

"Then should I have a lawyer?"

"You should consult a lawyer on that."

After further unprofitable exchange, Marvin took his leave and crossed the few short yards of grass to the Law School. His Critical Legal Studies friend, at his desk in his shirt sleeves, his blue blazer over a chair, was emphatic.

"Of course you need a lawyer."

"I should consult him during my testimony?"

"Certainly not. He shouldn't be at the table with you. That implies guilt, and properly so. He should follow things from a little way back."

"Suppose I go wrong on something?"

"There's nothing can be done about that."

"Will you come?"

He promised to catch an early plane down on the morning of the hearing.

On an insufferably warm afternoon in early summer, Marvin and Marjie flew to Washington and, as was their habit, housed themselves in a large room in the Hay-Adams looking out on Lafayette Park and the White House. The scene conveyed a feeling of calm and serenity that, on the whole, they did not share.

.   .   .

In the English-speaking countries all matters bearing on either the writing or enforcing of the law must go forward in the presence of the proper wood — always dark oak, darker mahogany or some reputable imitation in plywood. The furniture, the other fixtures and the paneling must all be suitably depressing as well. So it was that morning. The hearing room of the House Banking Committee, as in abbreviation it is called, was somber and superficially impressive. From above, portraits of noted past chairmen — Wright Patman of Texas, Henry Reuss of Wisconsin — gave watchful eye to the proceedings.

As Marvin and Marjie arrived, the seats were filling up with the day's audience, part of the large Washington leisure class that is closely concerned with public affairs. Each morning its members scan *The Washington Post* to see where on Capitol Hill they can expect to find the most interesting approach to public theatre. Their expectations are often defeated.

Also present when the Marvins got there were three television cameras, crews and connecting cables, and a half-dozen reporters were seated at the press table staring open-mouthed at the ceiling, some of them tapping pencils on their teeth. Committee members were beginning to occupy their seats back of the high bench; the staff had already taken up tutorial positions on the chairs behind them.

Eventually the chairman arrived and called the session to order. Marvin moved to his place at the witness table; a stenotypist at a small desk in front looked up at him and then at the chairman; the hearing got under way.

The chairman thanked Marvin for his cooperation. The purpose of the hearing was purely to gain information — a better understanding of Professor Marvin's financial operations, about which there had been considerable recent newspaper comment. The purpose was not to criticize in any way what he did with his money, a matter on which there had also been considerable comment. That, so long as within the law — there was a pause for emphasis here — so long as clearly within the law, was entirely Professor Marvin's own business. He asked Marvin if he would like to make any opening statement.

Marvin replied as Professor Grierson had advised by saying that he would like to cooperate with the committee "to the fullest"; he was there to answer their questions; he knew their purpose was to inform and seek information. He concluded by speaking again of his desire to cooperate.

The senior Republican on the committee being absent, the second-ranking party member took over. "You are an economist, I believe, Professor. Could you outline for the committee your principal interest and your qualifications in this field?"

Marvin nodded and responded with an account of his work to date on the theory of refrigerator pricing and immediately related issues. This, again following the Grierson instruction, took some time. The congressman listened with an evident show of attention but finally said, "You are also involved in the stock market, are you not?"

"I am," Marvin replied, "but I regard that as an extracurricular activity. It is not my basic area of teaching and research."

"Tell us about your stock market operations."

There was an interruption. A young congressman at the far end of the bench said, "Mr. Chairman, could I intervene for a question bearing on what the witness has just told the committee?"

The chairman nodded agreement.

"I have a fairly big Frigidaire plant in my district. It employs a couple of thousand men and women when everyone is working, and I wonder how you see the prospect of Japanese and Korean competition in this industry, Professor?"

Marvin answered again in detail, and, buzzers having sounded, the committee adjourned for a vote. The House was in early session that day. When the hearing reconvened, the ranking Republican was present, and he took up his colleague's question on the stock market.

Marvin replied as so often before: "I undertake to identify and measure unjustified optimism and pessimism, speculative euphoria and undue depression in securities' prices, and then act on my findings."

"That sounds very reasonable. Could I ask you to give an example?"

"As one example, I some time ago gave a certain amount of attention to Texas banks and savings and loan associations."

"You sold some of them short?"

"Yes."

"Then don't your operations imply a serious absence of faith in the American free enterprise system? You apparently sit around trying to find out what is going wrong. Un-American, I suppose some would say."

"I try to make money," said Marvin. "That seems to me very much in the American spirit."

"I can't wholly agree," said the congressman. "We want forward-looking businessmen and financiers in this country. Those who look on the bright side of things. That's the way this country was built."

There were several nods of approval. The congressman looked at the television cameras and smiled.

A senior Democrat then questioned Marvin as to the details of his work — IRAT and his means for measuring the errors of optimism and pessimism. As ever, Marvin's answers were precise, detailed and very technical. The congressman gave every indication of understanding. He did not nor did any of the others in the room. Marvin was then asked about any past association with Ivan Boesky or the great Wall Street house of Drexel Burnham Lambert. Of this he assured the committee there had been none.

Two or three committee members surrendered their turn to ask questions, and a lean-faced man with a strong Texas accent looked down on Marvin. He had not been briefed on the limits of the investigation.

"Professor, you seem to have a lot of spare money."

Marvin tried to convey the impression of reacting calmly.

"What I want to know is why are you usin' it to defeat me and my good frien's here in Congress? Who in the hell — strike that — who in Hades ever gave you that idea?"

It was the question for which Marvin had been waiting.

Mentally, and out loud to Marjie, he had rehearsed his answer.

"I'm sorry, Congressman; we're not trying to defeat anyone. We're only trying to keep things fair. Establish a level playing field, as it's called. I'm sure you've heard the expression. If there is money for a piece of legislation, we want money on the other side against it. You can't really object to that, can you?"

"I sure as hell do, and so does everyone on this here committee."

There were barely perceptible murmurs of agreement.

A young congressman held up his hand. "I don't object, Congressman. I don't take any PAC money myself. I got the word on that from my former senator. Proxmire, you may recall."

Attention, markedly adverse, shifted sharply to the young man from Wisconsin.

Two other committee members asked Marvin if his exploitation of irrationality was not out of step with the system. One called it "a kind of subversion of free enterprise." Reading from a question handed him by an assistant, a third asked if Marvin knew of the Rational Expectations school of economists. Marvin replied that he did.

"Don't they represent the good sound mainstream of American economic thought?"

"I'm not sure," said Marvin. "There is something to be said for identifying error — a stock or a bond too low or too high — and then applying a correction in the form of purchases or sales."

"That seems reasonable to me," said the congressman, "but shouldn't you then just give the profits to charity?

The Red Cross? The United Way? Even the ACLU, for God's sake? It's what one should do with money that doesn't smell quite right."

The nods of approval verged on the emphatic.

Marvin thought it better not to respond.

A legislator of marked scholarly appearance now leaned over to the microphone before him.

"Professor, you're acquainted with the work of Professor Samuelson? You know his textbook?"

"Yes, certainly."

"You agree that he's a good economist?"

"Certainly. The most distinguished of his generation."

"Then could you tell me why his textbook makes no mention of that IRAT, as you call it — that index of yours? I had no memory of it from my own college days, and I had the Library of Congress check the matter this morning. No mention."

"Perhaps one day it will be in all the textbooks. Until now I have considered it a largely private matter. Perhaps I could explain it more fully."

The chairman intervened in alarm. "I'm afraid we're running short of time."

The hearing came to an end.

The television crews had long since packed up and left. Two newspapermen cornered Marvin for private interviews, asking questions that had previously been asked by the committee.

. . .

Marvin and Marjie were taken to lunch at the House restaurant by the young Wisconsin congressman. Their lawyer, approving generally of Marvin's performance, walked over with them and then disappeared on some business of his own.

Both the Marvins thought that amid the noisy clatter there were some hostile looks from the surrounding tables. The likelihood of this the congressman affirmed. Later, their airline flight having in the normal course of operations been canceled, they talked it over while waiting to double-shuttle via New York to Boston.

"We've been fooling ourselves," said Marjie. "Everything so far — women in executive jobs, South Africa, those professorships — has been too easy. To do good you must be disliked. Make people angry. That's what counts. That's what we learned today."

"They were fairly polite," said Marvin.

"Don't fool yourself," said Marjie. "They were pretty mad at you, and that's proof that we're now finally doing something."

"I'm not really looking for trouble," said Marvin.

"You never are," said Marjie.

· 15 ·

THE TAKEOVER

THE PRCs had a good reception at Harvard and then across the country. In the days following his testimony Marvin was congratulated thoughtfully by friends and neighbors. Newsmen sought him out as never before. So did local television crews. With an eye to getting attention for the new committees, Marvin responded in a modestly cooperative way and even made a slightly disappointing appearance on the *Today* show. Marjie also made herself available to the media.

It was an election year, and from New England, California and even from a few politically resistant constituencies in the Deep South requests for PRC funds came in. When the elections were held, there were some notable victories. A number of them would have occurred anyway — some retirements were known to be long overdue — but, whether rightly or not, the PRCs got the credit. Inevitably their success added to the negative attitudes of many of the incumbents who had survived on

Capitol Hill; however, even in Washington, the Political
Rectitude Committees gained approval. Electoral pun-
dits — those who, having predicted one election cor-
rectly, are about to be wrong on the next — saw them
as a major factor in future contests. The Marvins' house was now added to Longfellow's
as an attraction for the tourist buses on Brattle Street, and
they themselves were occasionally pointed out as the occupants. When Marvin attended faculty meetings, as
somewhat infrequently he did, it was expected that he
would speak; that was the conceded prerogative of professors of extraterritorial fame. He chose to maintain silence, as also, with rare exceptions, he did at meetings of
the economics department. His classes were well attended, although with the usual disappointment that he
confined himself so rigorously to the issues that reflected
his professional competence. A lecture in the ARCO
Forum of the Kennedy School of Government on "International Rhythms in the Air Conditioning Industry"
had a capacity audience but was unenthusiastically applauded when he was through.

.   .   .

Much as he might have wished to the contrary, an increasing amount of Marvin's time had to be allotted to
his personal affairs. Cycles of optimism and cosmological
gloom persisted, and IRAT continued to identify the aberrations with admirable effectiveness. That effectiveness,
at least, was not a matter for concern. And there was the
beneficial effect of the growing number of hitchhikers
who had been identified as a problem by George Mozart
and Alois Hague and who still enthusiastically matched

Marvin's every sale or purchase and thus further ensured his success. Marvin was not in danger of losing; had he been in danger, with the hitchhikers rushing aboard he still could not lose. His problem was now somewhat different.

It was what he should do with the money.

The Harvard rescue had, in the not very long run, been financially rewarding; the peace professorships were a minor retail transaction rich in moral satisfaction, relatively small in cost; the PRCs required more money, but even their claims could in no way keep up with the revenues being received.

At Andover, Massachusetts, where Phillips Academy shares the local terrain with the offices of the Internal Revenue Service, the arrival of the Marvins' forms and payments was an occasion for discreetly expressed awe, and the latter extended all the way to those who fed the voracious computers and saw the unending printouts at the great center of record and surveillance in Martinsburg, West Virginia. What remained for the Marvins was, nonetheless, far more than they had ever anticipated.

There was only one course; that was to move on from trading to investment — to put money into the government bonds born of the still persisting federal deficit or into the stocks and bonds of stable, promising companies with low IRATs and put it there to stay. This course did not exclude investment in the big Boston, New York, Chicago and far western banks. At Citibank, Chase Manhattan and now out in San Francisco at the Bank of America, to the eccentricities of which Marvin owed so much in initial research and innovation and which was now doing better, the appearance of his name as a serious stockholder was a source of marked interest, prompting inquiry as to his ultimate purpose and sometimes some concern. These did not diminish as it became known that Marvin might be moving in on General Electric.

. . .

The rumor had its origin in the Marvins' own household. Marvin and Marjie were again sitting out on the back terrace on Brattle Street. The autumn colors were strong, the wind soft. The twins were at school. It was a short break after a late lunch.

"Why don't we just take over General Electric? It would be something different. Make it a model of business and social ethics." It was, as ever, Marjie who took the initiative.

"GE's very big," said Marvin, "and heavily in the defense industry. Do you want to be providing the electronic gear for the Stealth bomber or the headlights for the cruise missile?"

"Sure, why not? Let those war plants be owned by people who are interested in peace. Anyhow, General Electric makes a lot of other things too. Dishwashers. Diagnostic imaging systems for hospitals. Maybe microwave ovens. Even some of your refrigerators. We owe it to them; remember that nest egg down in Maine. GE helped get us started."

"Most of those things are outside my specialty. They have nothing to do with refrigeration price theory."

"You know perfectly well," said Marjie, "that you don't need to know anything about the things a company produces before you buy it. I've read that those great takeover people — Pickens, Icahn, Campeau — sometimes don't even know what all their targets make or do. And you know about NBC, after all."

"Not very much. I did do that *Today* show."

"There are times I think you have a relentlessly small mind. Professor Solow over at MIT said it: economists are 'determined little thinkers.' Can't you see the big picture here?"

"I get your point — I guess. A giant corporation that is a major producer for the Pentagon becomes a strong force for reason. Tom Brokaw, the powerful voice of peace. Is that what you're saying?"

Marjie ignored the slightly bantering tone. "What's wrong with that?"

"I think we should start with something smaller, more manageable. Maybe begin with Special Electric."

"What do you know about it?"

"It comes right after Westinghouse in size. Advanced electronics; consumer products. They have a freezer line, which is how I first heard of them. I expect they do components for the Stealth and B-1 as well. And they have a chain of TV stations. They're also supposed to be getting into cable."

"I think you're missing the really big one," said Marjie, "but let's go ahead."

It was because of this conversation that the rumor got started about General Electric. Lunching a few days later with Professor Grierson at Cambridge's Harvest restaurant, Marvin told his colleague that he was just back from a trip to Schenectady, where he had been consulting on next year's durable product prices. Grierson had sought the lunch to pump Marvin a bit on the refrigerator growth prospect, and in discussion Marvin mentioned casually that Marjie had wanted him "to take a position in General Electric." The news evidently went directly to GE headquarters and after a major exercise in magnification traveled on. On Wall Street it became established truth; there was a small blip in General Electric stock, mild alarm in Fairfield and Schenectady. The blip Marvin didn't notice, for he was concentrating his attention on Special Electric — in corporate and financial parlance, SPELCO.

This would be another turning point in the Marvins' family history.

.   .   .

Marvin added carefully to his SPELCO holdings. This time he did not want the responsive price increase which inevitably followed the illicit spread of the news that he was buying. He solicited the cooperation of the trust departments of two banks, one in Boston, one in New York, where both his personal stock holdings and his deposits now induced a marked deference. "Professor Marvin will be in this morning; ask him to stay for lunch." Out of funds they held for him and in as close an approach to secrecy as the higher realms of finance allow, they began accumulating the stock on his behalf.

The operation went smoothly, with no grave disturbance to the market. Presently, and sooner than anyone could have imagined, the day of 13D approached; 13D is the requirement of the Securities and Exchange Commission that anyone who has acquired an appreciable holding in a company, 5 percent in fact, must declare whether he or she intends passive investment or a bid for potential control.

Marvin came out of the shadows; through the agency

of the greatly respectable Morgan Guaranty, now his principal investment banker, he affirmed his intention to control. This he followed with an offer, expiring six weeks hence, of an advantage of around 30 percent over the present price of the stock. Thereafter the offer would lapse and so, presumably, the price. Marvin's own resources, supplemented by some modest bank support, were sufficient for the bid.

Across the country somnambulant pension fund managers, avowedly perceptive mutual fund managers, bank advisers to the aged, financial experts for the Ford and MacArthur foundations, the treasurers of Amherst and Williams colleges, the Harvard Management Company, came forward with recommendations as to holding or selling SPELCO that they were often profoundly unqualified to make. The reports flowing in to the Mass. Avenue offices and to Brattle Street were generally favorable. The stock was being acquired at a wholly acceptable rate.

At SPELCO there was naturally concern at the prospect of a new and inevitably intrusive owner. It could mean the end of a secure and quiet life for the company's managers. There was talk among them of a leveraged buyout. Funds would be borrowed from the big banks, and the great investment houses would be recruited to sell junk bonds. From the proceeds, management would purchase the voting stock, and thus control would remain in its own hands. One of the more imaginative of the investment banking houses, in pursuit of its ultimate sales goal, planned a large evening at the Beverly Hills Hotel, assembled its salesmen and wealthier clients and alerted a corps of seemingly ascetic but available women who could apply their own accomplished sales pressure.

Marvin had little difficulty in countering the move against him. He notified the banks in which he now had a substantial interest that he would oppose any advance of credit for any such purpose. And word went similarly to the more reputable investment brokers. Montgomery Marvin was no longer a man who could be ignored. He had money and the access to more. This was widely known. Here, unmistakably, the positive power of wealth.

At the same time he sent assurances to SPELCO's exceptionally attentive managers that, matters of general policy apart, he did not intend to interfere with their daily routine. Their golden parachutes, designed to ensure those tranquil years in Hobe Sound, would never need to open. As far as the electric generators, the electric fans and the toasters were concerned, the managers would still be fully in charge.

The appearance of a new corporate raider — a professor of economics, no less — was, as might be imagined, serious news. When Marvin passed through the Faculty Club dining room after his late morning lecture, the conversation often stopped entirely. He was featured on the business pages of newspapers around the nation and occasionally on the front pages as well. Reporters were assigned full time to his activities. After his brief public availability when the PRCs were being launched, Marvin had, however, returned to his preferred reticence. A well-spoken young woman at the Mass. Avenue offices spent nearly all her time graciously declining requests for interviews while promising to forward messages.

In general, the response to his new initiative was favorable. There was warm praise in *The Wall Street Journal* for this latest manifestation of the spirit of entrepreneurship. Both *Newsweek* and *Time* contemplated cover stories; only Marvin's reluctance to be interviewed on the takeover and thus to supply the essential copy forced them to abstain. Both weeklies did write thoughtfully of "a new style" in American corporate finance. NOW THE ACADEMIC YUPPIE was the headline on a compelling profile of the Marvins in *The Village Voice,* and a photographer for *People* magazine, ruthlessly intruding on the property next door, got a touching photograph of Marvin trimming the rose bushes in the back yard on Brattle Street.

In the Congress the PRCs still rankled, and nothing to do with their sponsor was left unexamined. But even there criticism was, for the moment, muted. A few liberals now owed their election to the Political Rectitude Committees, and conservatives had as always to make overtures to their faith. The takeover, whatever the auspices, was just another example of the benign course of the free enterprise system; one should never be distracted by its occasional wayward tendencies. A scholarly Utah senator rose in the Senate chamber to say that there are "sometimes deep and seemingly inexplicable currents in the broad and beneficial stream that is our economic system. We know, however, that in the end that rush of water is guided and controlled by the invisible hand that, in the absence of government interference, assures us always of the best refreshment of what would otherwise be a parched and barren land." In the same session Edward Kennedy of Massachusetts, while expressing concern over the disturbing concentration of economic power resulting from corporate takeovers and leveraged buyouts, said that if this process had to go forward, it could not be in better hands than those of Montgomery

Marvin. He received permission to put in *The Congressional Record* a speech by Professor Grierson of Harvard carefully analyzing this whole tendency. The White House affirmed its strong support of a hands-off policy where financial markets were concerned.

The SEC, however, continued its study of IRAT and the torrential flood of orders that followed any initial sale or purchase by Marvin.

While the discussion proceeded, Marvin consolidated his hold on SPELCO. During a special meeting of the stockholders, at which he was now nearly alone, he announced that any member of the board of directors with nominal holdings who so desired could remain; the board had not for some years taken a stand on any issue in opposition to management. Added only would be Win, to whom some stock had been assigned, and a professor from the Harvard Business School, a member of several other corporate boards, whose teaching specialty was business ethics and its moral implications. Subject to policy changes that would become clear in the course of the next weeks, pretty much everything at the company would continue as before.

· · ·

"We seem to be in the headlines again," said Marvin as he sat down to breakfast with Marjie and the twins. He passed over a folded copy of *The Wall Street Journal*. The editorial spoke of his takeover of Special Electric. "There are those who will criticize this latest example of what the uninformed call corporate raiding. We, not surprisingly, dissent. Admittedly, Mr. Marvin is a liberal; with his personal political views we do not agree. But as an expression of the entrepreneurial spirit so manifest in our time, he should be welcomed onto the industrial scene. He is in the tradition of Commodore Vanderbilt, John D. Rockefeller and J. Pierpont Morgan. Their example lives on."

"I have some difficulty in seeing you as the Vanderbilt reincarnation," said Marjie, "but we got this company for a purpose. Let's get on with it."

. . .

Jove, it is said, strikes his mountain builders down not when they begin but when another stone would crown their work. This the Marvins did not know. The time had come for them to specify the rules which as owners of SPELCO they believed should govern operations. Jove awaited.

· 16 ·

THE RECKONING

"THAT WAS a very dull meeting. Now I understand why executive salaries are so high. Boredom. I'm glad we're going to liven things up."

It was Marjie who spoke; she, Win and Marvin were on the corporate jet coming back from Stamford to Boston's Logan Airport, their Business School colleague having gone on to Passaic, New Jersey, for another board meeting. All four had taken the train down to SPELCO headquarters, but the Vice-President for Executive Services had insisted that they return by plane. Some corporate amenities, they learned, are obligatory.

"I think we should take things gradually," said Marvin. "We need to feel our way."

"I've heard that before," said Marjie. "But we must have some civilized action at the company for Win to watch."

The conversation was suspended briefly as the co-pilot appeared with drinks, hors d'oeuvres, sandwiches, salad,

ice cream and fruit. "Not really a meal," he said pleasantly. "We do have coffee and some liqueurs."

When he had gone, Marjie returned to an earlier conversation. "I thought we bought SPELCO for a purpose.
Surely we're going to put it to some use."

"There are still some minority stockholders. We must
consider their interests."

"You're beginning to sound like any other tycoon. It
must be this jet."

. . .

The directives that Marvin issued to management de-
tailing the policies of the new owners were, in fact, fairly
modest. They reflected more the shadow than the substance of recent political developments — scandals in military procurement, questionable weapons development,
the changed international scene.

SPELCO would no longer hire lobbyists, commonly
called consultants, to advise and persuade the Pentagon
and guide the flow of Defense Department contracts to
the company. No longer would its executives be on the
other side of the revolving door. It would take what
orders came or what it received in straightforward bids.

It would not bid on, or accept, any contract for any
military purpose that its own scientists and engineers regarded as manifestly unnecessary, unsound or presumptively insane. Participation in Star Wars — the Strategic
Defense Initiative — was an obvious example. No peb-
bles in space. Such work must surely be destructive of
technical and scientific morale; serious men and women
should not be engaged on tasks that are patently unpro-
ductive. And, in the nature of the case, such employment
is also temporary; in weeks, months or perhaps years it

comes to be seen by all concerned as foolish, and then, even with the strongest military and political support, it can continue only a few years more. And, of course, it wastes public money.

Finally, the company would identify and invest modestly in its own future as that reflected the larger picture of the country and humankind. Four percent of its net earnings from Defense contracts would be set aside each year to find and develop new civilian opportunities. As and when peace came or might come, the company would be prepared or, in any case, it would not be held by rigid necessity to its military business. The 4 percent was a compromise; Marvin and Win had thought 2, and Marjie had said 10.

These directives spelled out policy for the company itself. A less seriously astringent communication went to the television stations. It would henceforth be SPELCO's wish that equal time be accorded persons and programs that spoke for the peace movement. As news came on the air of the Minuteman, the Midgetman and the MX and on Pentagon briefings and budgets, there would also be reports of the reaction of the Union of Concerned Scientists, the Council for a Livable World, SANE/ FREEZE and the Center for Defense Information. The work of those worthy organizations on behalf of peace and arms control would be discussed as well. No compulsion was here implied; this was a reminder only of the American tradition of fairness and equal access to the public eye and ear.

Marvin made another trip to Stamford in order to go over this guidance with the company management. It was well received.

"It's a pleasure," said the president and CEO, "to be

associated with enlightened, forward-looking, progressive, thought-provoking ideas of genuine national significance." More privately to his immediate associates he offered the thought that the new owner was maybe a trifle flaky.

. . .

The Marvin policy statements did not remain a secret, and SPELCO's Senior Vice-President for Defense-Related Public Affairs was questioned at length about them at his regular news conference in Washington. In his reply he generally confirmed the company's new guidelines and reported what the CEO had said to Marvin in approval.

Such approval was by no means universal. In architecturally sordid buildings extending out from Washington to the Beltway and beyond, in small plush offices replete with inscribed photographs affirming or alleging past public service, there was sharply expressed anger over the rejection of consultants. It was an intrusion on the well-established order of business; it cast doubt on the legitimacy of the means of livelihood of men who, on modest public salaries, had once given their best to the public interest in the hope and knowledge of future private reward. Highly critical comment was made to members of Congress and more discreetly to the press.

There was also an adverse reaction from senior Defense officials and the administration generally. SPELCO's decision to take no more contracts for projects regarded as foolish put the Strategic Defense Initiative, which was already under fire, even more obviously at risk; the company's Laser Division in Midland, Texas, had research-and-development contracts running to something over $30 million. Special Electric had designed the electronics and also some of the flotation gear for the Bradley fighting vehicle, and there was question as to whether those contracts would continue.

"This company by its arrogance is putting the very essentials of our nation's defenses at risk" was the statement issued by an Assistant Deputy Under Secretary of the Army.

"An astonishing and egregious exercise in scientific arrogance" was the view expressed by an assistant to a senior aide of the Science Adviser to the President, who asked to remain anonymous.

"Arrogant," said the head of the Office of Management and Budget.

And there was one even grimmer comment. "Naturally we are investigating the motives involved here," said a spokesman for the FBI. "Beyond that I cannot say."

． ． ．

The media response was more temperate. In a strong editorial *The New York Times* found much to be said both for and against the action of the company, though, on balance, the editors seemed slightly to question its wisdom.

One afternoon when Eldon Carroll saw Marvin coming down Massachusetts Avenue, he followed him into Harvard Square, through the Harvard Coop and finally into its book department across the narrow street behind the main store.

"Aren't you pretty much just setting yourself in judgment on military matters, Professor Marvin?" The speed of the pursuit had kept Carroll from thinking his question through in more detail.

"No, I think not."

"Why not?"

"We are only being guided away from what the very best people here and at MIT say is unworkable, silly, maybe a little demented. We save the government money and keep our company out of absurd contracts that could one day be canceled."

"Is that all you have to say?"

"What more is there to say?"

Carroll changed the subject. "Do you intend any more takeovers in this field? General Dynamics? General Electric? Westinghouse?" The question was a long shot.

"I have no such plans."

"I can take that as a denial?"

"Absolutely."

Marvin turned in a determined way to look at the shelf that held the newest economics books.

Craftwin didn't think it much of a story but gave it a front-page box nonetheless. NEW SPELCO OWNER DEFENDS SDI BOYCOTT was the headline; the article went on to say that Marvin had no plans for General Dynamics.

.   .   .

There was also criticism of the decision to allot a share of SPELCO's weapons revenues to peacetime production, although it was conceded that with the Pentagon no longer under siege from the consultants, other business would be needed. The negative comments, whether emanating from the Congress (where the chairman of the House Armed Services Committee was thoughtfully articulate), the White House, the Secretary of Defense or, in more muted terms, from a dozen voices in the Pentagon, were surprisingly similar. SPELCO's action implied that weapons expenditures and weapons production were in some measure conditional, that this was a business which with a better world situation might come to an end. This was held to be a supremely dangerous view and one that attacked a basic principle. The American commitment to a strong defense is no casual thing; it is permanent and enduring. Admittedly, there had been an easing of tension on the international scene. A Soviet ambition to take over and run anything as intricate as the West German or Japanese economy was coming to seem somewhat improbable. So also its passion, which was shared by many Americans, for mutually assured destruction. None of this, however, could be an excuse for relaxation in weapons devlopment. That had a need and a life of its own. That need and that life were threatened by SPELCO's ill-advised, irresponsible preparation for peacetime production.

. . .

Finally, some disapproval was registered even at Harvard. Marvin's takeover of SPELCO was taken calmly at the university. His outside activities were certainly a matter for much discussion, but he was known to be a serious scholar, and even the most serious faculty members have extracurricular interests. The only unforgivable aberration is to concentrate too exclusively on making money. Marvin was undoubtedly making a great deal, but he was using it for good purposes. The peace professorships. The PRCs. Eventually, however, one decidedly stern local rebuke did get considerable attention.

It was made on a pleasant autumn evening when Marvin and Marjie picked up Win and strolled down Brattle

Street through the youthful pedestrian throngs of Harvard Square, then down John F. Kennedy Street (still called Boylston Street by the older and more recalcitrant Cantabrigians) to the Kennedy School of Government. There they found relatively obscure seats off the staircase overlooking the auditorium of the ARCO Forum. The topic for the evening, which had drawn them to the meeting, was relevant to their present concerns. As so often in these matters, undue originality had been avoided; it was "New Challenges in National Security Policy."

There was another reason for their attendance. Marvin, with all his activities, was a little weary. When he had gone to similar earlier sessions, he had not found them to be intellectually taxing; a rewarding convention governing all such subject matter excluded new and mentally oppressive thoughts. This evening was meant to be one for relaxation. Things turned out rather differently.

The speaker was a rotund, intense scholar, a former Deputy Under Secretary of State known for his forthright energy of assertion, who was now teaching part time at the Georgetown Center for Strategic and International Studies. Coming to the podium, he remarked on the undoubted sensitivity "here in Cambridge" of the views he would express but stressed his own higher obligation to what he called, with a slight note of self-approval, "the unvarnished truth." Brushing back his thinning hair, bringing his round face alarmingly close to the microphone, he then launched into his address.

"We live," he said, "in a time of exceptional peril." He paused briefly as if to allow his audience to come abreast of the thought.

Continuing, he said, "When international tensions are

high and increasing, we can count on the American people to respond. But in recent months these tensions have been easing. And here, I fear, is the danger — the mortal danger. It is that our people will now relax. They will fail to see the need for continuing vigilance and unrelenting commitment. They will fail to see that only by preparation for seemingly inevitable conflict can we ensure international peace and tranquillity."

He paused again and then, his face implacably stern, went on. "I am forced to stress this point tonight here at Harvard, for in this community, as you know, can be found the ownership and directing force of one of our most critically important producers of modern defensive and deterrent weapons. That firm, we hear, is planning conversion from weapons production and weapons development to peacetime pursuits. Such an action I must condemn. Such an action we must all condemn. We must all of us see our national defense as independent of the vagrant tides of international relations. It is a pillar of our power; as a pillar it must stand against any and every calm and every wind."

Another pause, and this time he allowed himself a trace of a smile.

"It has been said that our military and weapons policy is not for hawks, not for doves, but for owls. With this I cannot agree. The true metaphor is the eagle soaring over the troubled world scene. Let no one cripple its wings."

When he was finished, a panel of scholars took over for comment and discussion. There were expressions of both approval and dissent, and eventually the moderator said in summation, "As so often in these matters, truth undoubtedly is to be found halfway between, a blend of what seems right and wrong."

Marvin, Marjie and Win had not stayed for the discussion. When the speech was over, they had gone quietly down the stairway and out into the street, but they did not escape unnoticed. The next day *The Harvard Crimson*, which had become increasingly relaxed in its language, had as its headline ECONOMICS PROFESSOR HEARS HIMSELF ASS-KICKED. WALKS OUT EARLY ON KSG DEBATE.

Even with that, however, the mood in the university as a whole remained generally uncritical. At the long table several spoke up for Marvin; McCrimmon himself was in only mild dissent. An anonymous grant in support of work on new horizons in psychometrics had, it was thought, somewhat mellowed his views. Marvin neither confirmed nor denied that one of his corporations was its source.

. . .

A night or two after the lecture Marvin and Marjie discussed their situation before going off to sleep in their large four-poster bed.

"It's really going our way," said Marjie. "That twerp from Georgetown showed how alarmed they are. I just heard that Jeane Kirkpatrick may have helped him with several early drafts of his speech."

"We may be running into more trouble than we know," said Marvin. "I showed you that story in the *Globe*."

"Taking over General Dynamics? That would be a wonderful idea. Why not McDonnell Douglas too? Maybe Boeing?"

"It would be too much too soon. There is real danger here. The whole thing came up because our friend Carroll asked me about General Dynamics."

"What did you tell him?"

"I denied it, and that naturally led people to think there was a story."

.   .   .

The General Dynamics rumor was discussed in precincts far beyond its board room. At the company itself there were consultations with lawyers and attention to poison pills, parachutes and the possibility here too of a leveraged buyout. Predictably Marvin's denial was a special source of anxiety.

The concern extended on into the Pentagon and to both of the Armed Services committees on Capitol Hill. If SPELCO was possible, why not General Dynamics, Raytheon or, God forbid, IBM? The weapons industry was surprisingly vulnerable; it could pass into the wrong hands — into the hands of people with a fugitive, perhaps even subversive, belief in peace, not war. Although everyone should respect laissez-faire, laissez-passer, the basic integrity of free enterprise, the innate wisdom of the financial markets, there could be limits.

The thought deepened and enlarged, but, in the end, it was not decisive. Gathering force elsewhere was the wind, perhaps more precisely the hurricane, that would sweep in on the Marvins with disastrous effect.

· 17 ·

THE TURN

IT WAS, they came later to know, ownership of the
SPELCO television stations that did it. These did not
constitute a reputable network in the manner of CBS,
NBC or ABC. They operated individually, subject only
to the general supervision of the corporation, most notably on the matter of earnings. No classical voice as of
Murrow or Cronkite, no modern voice as of Brokaw,
Jennings or Rather, informed, guided or, on occasion,
stirred the multitude with the day's events. Each station
made its own independent way. National and international news came almost entirely from the wire services;
local news was gathered by astonishingly diligent crews
who could be seen of an evening interviewing local politicians of agreed inconsequence or invading some distressed and desolate home to view the devastating tragedy
that had befallen its occupants that day.

Marvin's new guidelines on how peace and the Pentagon were to be reported were calmly received and,

perhaps predictably, did not long remain a secret. They were mentioned over the air with seeming approval on the SPELCO stations; they were picked up with keen interest by the national press; they were discussed with sensitive indignation by the network news teams. The eventual reaction was far stronger than the Marvins could have foreseen.

Conservatives were particularly severe, for it seemed clear that grave public principles were involved. "Television is being turned against the defense of the Republic," said *The Wall Street Journal*. "Commie stuff," said *The New York Post*. "Subversion of everything this nation stands for," said the Utah senator. A North Carolina colleague took the Senate floor to say, "We must now face the serious question as to who should be allowed to own our communications media and have access to our air waves. There are many people and institutions whose ownership we do not fear — whom I do not fear — who have had my willing participation in the past. But it is now relentlessly clear that there are some exceptions to the American free enterprise design, exceptions that could bring the voice of subversion into every living room in our land. When Americans exercise their property rights under free enterprise, nearly all of them do so for the common good. But now we see that some of them do it for the highly exceptional evil. This is a distinction which our free enterprise system must now make. Let us get on to the task of making it."

The speech was made to a Senate audience of more than a dozen members and was seen on Cable News Network. The senator was congratulated warmly by three or four of his colleagues, including, notably, two who were under threat from the PRCs. Staff members in both houses went to work on the appropriate legislation.

The responsible liberal reaction, on the other hand, was more tempered. SPELCO was a very large corporation and with all else an arms manufacturer. Should a weapons firm have access to the privileged voice of television even for the best of purposes? And, in issuing formal written guidelines, wasn't the owner violating the essential principles of freedom of the press? Admittedly journalists may guess as to what the owner or owning corporation wants to hear and be so guided; self-censorship in all written and oral expression is, after all, normal and expected. But there is a line to be drawn. Free men and free women who write for a living must not be overtly told.

It was unnatural, in any case, for liberals to come to the defense of a very large corporation. Even if Marvin's instructions seemed quite sensible, they could be the cover for a deeper, perhaps insidious intent. "We are keeping all our fingers crossed," said Ralph Nader in a widely quoted comment. "There could be either more or less here than meets the eye." Common Cause was more positive in its approach. "Let us never be unduly negligent in regard to corporate control of the means of communication." *The New York Times,* on balance, was doubtful, its columnists evenly divided. *The Nation* gave its approval, but it too proclaimed a need for caution. That caution became concern when the conservative journal *National Review,* after deploring the general thrust of Marvin's guidelines, affirmed what its editor, Mr. William F. Buckley, Jr., called "the right of any and every American corporation to speak its mind."

·   ·   ·

It is not good in the American democracy to be without defenders. A bill was introduced in the House and Senate forbidding any corporation with more than a half-billion-dollar commitment to the arms industry to own a television station; only the major networks were exempted. The bill had the warm support of all who felt threatened by the PRCs or enjoyed the favor of the PACs and passed with substantial majorities in both houses. Signing the new law, the President said, "The legislation I approve today is another living expression of our support to the First Amendment. In its assurance of free, untrammeled speech it removes our defense industry, the men and women of our armed forces, all who so serve our country, from the effects of ill-motivated, ill-spirited, unpatriotic propaganda. I am today assured by the Federal Communications Commission that enforcement of this law will be prompt, complete, thoroughgoing, vigorous and unrelenting in the fullest sense of all those words."

In the White House press room this was thought one of the strongest, most articulate statements to have come from the presidential writing staff in some months. Partly in consequence, the national media reaction was generally favorable. Invited to go on the *Today* show again, this time to discuss the effect of the new restrictions on SPELCO, Marvin declined. In fact, he had another, more pressing matter on his mind.

. . .

It was the SEC. Once again the Commission's lawyers had come to Cambridge, this time for an appointment at Marvin's Massachusetts Avenue offices which he was warned not to miss. Accompanying them, in a slightly threadbare suit, checked shirt and bow tie, was a sternvisaged man with a substantial briefcase, from which he pulled an inch-thick stack of computer printouts. A short and austere press release at the beginning explained that, in a civil complaint, Marvin was being charged with violation of the securities laws. IRAT, it had been determined, involved an illegal manipulation of the securities markets based on privileged information. While the use of inside information in the older sense was not alleged, the IRAT measurement of irrationality "and the actions proceeding therefrom" not only gave to the possessor, namely Marvin, an unfair advantage, but they were also used by others as inside information to the profit of those who had inside knowledge of Marvin's operations. The result, it was said, was "to have at one remove from illegal manipulation the effect of inside information based on that manipulation." In unfair competition with a certain winner, the inevitable losers were unfairly treated. Eventually the free market would be damaged, perhaps destroyed.

Applicable provisions of the Securities Exchange Act were cited at length. The intention to recover illegally acquired gains was made clear.

As before, Marvin's visitors expressed the thought that perhaps he would wish any further discussion to be in the presence of counsel. This time he agreed. They took their departure.

Marvin's lawyers, including his colleague in the blue blazer, urged him to protest the charges. They predicted success, and this view was shared by the noted Boston law firm of Bill and Marlow, to which he also turned in this emergency. Marjie was strongly for a challenge, but Marvin resisted. For perhaps the first time in their married life he was intransigent.

It was, he thought, decisive that there was legislation now pending in both the Senate and the House amending the securities laws in such a way as effectively to proscribe IRAT trading. It would allow continued trading on the more broadly based indexes such as the Standard & Poor's 500, but it specifically reinforced the SEC decision outlawing trading on the basis of any index of irrational expectations. There was known to be wide support for the bill. Again the hostility to the PRCs and again the wisdom and voice of the Oklahoma legislator, who in a series of highly repetitive speeches urged, as he had before, the unlikelihood of honesty accompanying the sudden acquisition of large sums of money. Going on to a more technical matter and with a clear sense of the originality of his position, he stressed the need to ensure that the securities markets were "on a level playing field," something that IRAT all too obviously did not allow. Corporate lobbyists and the Political Action Committees rallied in solid strength to support by necessary regulation the integrity of the free market.

When hearings were held on the legislation, Marvin was invited to attend. He declined. The bill passed after very little debate.

· · ·

All who spoke for the securities markets responded well to the suppression of Marvin's activities. Clearly his continued success meant that somewhere, somehow, there would be companionate losses. "This legislation," said the president of the New York Stock Exchange, "is a desirable, even necessary step on the path to intelligent, discriminating deregulation. That path is made wider and easier by this well-considered barrier, which halts and ar-

rests any destructive commitment to market irrationality."
Other financial comment was equally favorable. The
public at large was, as is often true in such matters, indifferent.

.   .   .

The Marvins, Marvin in particular, were thought to survive their reverses calmly. The Massachusetts Avenue
offices were quietly abandoned; the network of corporations that supported the PRCs, now no longer sustained
by a flush flow of funds, was disbanded. Congressional
incumbents could face the future with enhanced confidence.

Control of SPELCO was sacrificed when the Marvins
settled with the SEC. This time the CEO made it rather
less of a secret that he thought Marvin was flaky. He so
said, although strictly not for attribution, to the press. A
corps of consultants on military contracts was gradually
reassembled by the company; work on the Strategic Defense Initiative was resumed; a contract for electronics for
the Stealth bomber was sought and won; the conversion
set-aside was set aside. The broadcasting stations were
quietly released from their commitment to the peace organizations. None of this caused much discussion.

The settlement left Marvin with more than enough
money to retain the Brattle Street house and keep the
twins in Shady Hill School. All the computers but one
were packed up. The filing cabinets were stored away in
the cellar. Marjie had already taken down and folded up
the curtains bearing the monogram PPW.

.   .   .

There was reason why Marvin was less perturbed than might have been expected. For some time prior to the second coming of the SEC, the IRAT findings had shown themselves increasingly and disturbingly erratic. Of the cause Marvin was not in doubt. The congressional hearing, the SEC charges and the resulting press comment had sent a new message to the financial community. Contrary to all acceptable economic theory, countering all the established financial wisdom, euphoria leading on to collective insanity could exist, even on occasion be normal, in the great financial markets of the world. This, Marvin the pioneer had shown. And so the further thought had spread: money could be made from so assuming, as, by this somber economics professor, much money had been made.

Accordingly, imitators had now appeared; in a dozen investment houses pseudo-IRAT calculations had been made and passed on to an eager public. These had not necessarily made money, but they had introduced a new and erratic factor into the Marvin calculations. New computer programs would be needed — programs that allowed for the market effect of investment action based on erratic or erroneous assumptions, euphoria, error and mild insanity. This would be a formidable task. As Marvin confided one day to Win, it was more, along with his teaching and his regular research, than he felt disposed to undertake. And he had another more than modest recourse to money.

While denying him the now impaired guidance of IRAT, the SEC did not forbid his purchases or sales of securities in the manner and according to the right of any American citizen. These Marvin continued to make but now at random, selecting only the securities of smaller, more volatile companies. To avoid any suggestion that he might be favoring those with inside knowledge of his operations, he notified the SEC promptly of his action in each case and issued a short press release listing the company and the amounts involved. It was no fault of his that his actions, so revealed, brought a crowd of fellow travelers — hitchhikers once again, in the perhaps more acceptable idiom of the day.

Marvin's reputation for a quiet prescience in these matters, the IRAT collapse notwithstanding, was, it developed, as great as any in the land. The rush of the hitchhikers promptly and decisively bid up or bid down security values. And this ensured the success of Marvin's investments. Giving similar notice, he realized gains. Others tried to do so. In failing and accepting their losses, they further enhanced Marvin's reputation. It was his small pride that, having discovered and measured the role of manic behavior in the financial world, he was now, in a modest way, its source. He was sorry that his imitators lost the money that he made. For that there was no remedy.

.   .   .

In these days he had another visit from the SEC. Alois Hague stopped by the Brattle Street house. The Commission's computers still showed that imitating rush. Marvin took him on a tour of the now derelict rooms. No computers, no printers, one Macintosh apart. No eager assistants at work. He spoke of his own diligence in informing the Commission of his purchases and sales. Hague told Marvin that he was persuaded that all was well. "No problem," he said.

Marvin was free to continue inflicting losses on his

unknown imitators. This he did with only gradually diminishing effect.

Meanwhile he had also returned, gratefully, to academic life. His classes were now smaller, more intense; in many ways he found them more rewarding. A paper delivered that winter at the annual meeting of the American Economic Association at the New York Hilton on "Price Determination Under Equilibrium Conditions for Consumer Durables Assuming the Paradigms of Perfect Knowledge" aroused interest and was selected for publication in the *Proceedings*. Colleagues noted that in his professional concerns he was going several steps yet farther from his earlier specialization on the refrigerator and immediately related industries.

．　．　．

Harvard is proud of its ancient respect for civilized values. If, from time to time, a professor has lapsed from the expected standards of professional, marital or financial morality or has found himself involved with the Central Intelligence Agency, it is understood, and especially by the older professors at the long table, that these are not matters for excessive comment. This protection, particularly as regards his financial ventures and misadventures, now favored Marvin. There was also only restrained mention of Marjie's absence in Washington to work for better relations with Fidel Castro and of her frequent trips to Cuba. Almost no mention was made of Win's decision, her former husband now forgotten, to move in with Marvin and bring up her son along with the twins.

．　．　．

Over at the *Globe,* Craftwin having just retired with the honors properly accruing to a distinguished career, his successor, an unduly energetic young man named John Fitzgerald Passos, remembered one day the compelling story of Marvin's operations and thought the paper should tell its readers how things had turned out.

Eldon Carroll was unavailable; suffering from an unfortunate occupational hazard, he was spending a few weeks in an unpleasant alcohol rehabilitation clinic. The reporter who was his replacement went out to Cambridge and talked with Marvin, who told him of his new work on microwave ovens and other kitchen appurtenances and of a possible venture into television pricing. The next to be interviewed was Professor Grierson, now dean of the Faculty of Arts and Sciences, in his offices in the lovely University Hall. It was a dark day and so was the room. Dimly visible behind his desk, Grierson spoke warmly of Professor Marvin's commitment to serious academic endeavor and gave a barely comprehensible summary of his now expanded work on consumer durables. Finally, the man from the *Globe* went to see McCrimmon, whose secretary said he could not be disturbed. He returned to tell Passos there was no story.

.   .   .

One day at the beginning of the new academic year Marvin met Professor McCrimmon on the steps of Widener Library, by common consent the intellectual as well as the etymological center of the university.

"You seem to have had some setbacks since last we met," McCrimmon said in an unusually pleasant way.

"A few," said Marvin.

"I was sorry to hear it. I gather most of the trouble was over those peace professorships? And getting those top jobs for women? I also heard that you took a bath on the South African securities you picked up from the university."

"There were other problems," said Marvin.

"Anyway, you still have tenure. I hope you remember that I told you to get that first."

"I do, indeed."

"Well, don't give up," said McCrimmon. "I see in the *Crimson* that you're to be the head of this year's United Way drive. That's good."

"I intend to give it my best," said Marvin.

BOOKS BY JOHN KENNETH GALBRAITH

THE AFFLUENT SOCIETY

Galbraith's classic on the "economics of abundance" cuts to the heart of what economic security means (and doesn't mean) in today's world. With customary clarity, eloquence, and humor, Galbraith lays bare the hazards of individual and societal complacence about economic inequity.   ISBN 0-395-92500-2

THE ESSENTIAL GALBRAITH

The Essential Galbraith includes key selections from many of Galbraith's most important works — from *The Affluent Society* to *The Great Crash*. New introductions to each of the sections place the works in their historical moment and make clear their enduring relevance. This collection offers unparalleled access to the seminal writings of an extraordinary thinker.   ISBN 0-618-11963-9

THE GOOD SOCIETY: THE HUMANE AGENDA

This compact, tightly argued, and eloquent book is quintessential John Kenneth Galbraith. In defining the characteristics of a good society and creating the blueprint for a workable agenda, Galbraith allows for human weakness without compromising a humane culture.   ISBN 0-395-85998-0

THE GREAT CRASH, 1929

Of Galbraith's examination of the 1929 financial collapse, the *Atlantic Monthly* said: "Economic writings are seldom notable for their entertainment value, but this book is. [Galbraith] distills a good deal of sardonic fun from the whopping errors of the nation's oracles and the wondrous antics of the financial community."   ISBN 0-395-85999-9

NAME-DROPPING: FROM F.D.R. ON

With the literary skill that marks Galbraith as one of the most distinguished writers of our time, *Name-Dropping* charts the political landscape of the past sixty-five years. The famous economist offers an amusing, unsparing, witty account of the people he has known in this uniquely personal history of the century.   ISBN 0-618-15453-1

A TENURED PROFESSOR

John Kenneth Galbraith's *A Tenured Professor* is at once an intriguing tale of morality and a comic delight. Montgomery Martin, a Harvard economics professor, creates a stock forecasting model, which makes it possible for him to uncover society's hidden agendas. Hailed as "his wisest and wittiest" novel (*New York Times*), *A Tenured Professor* is an impudently satirical tale.   ISBN 0-618-15455-8

AVAILABLE IN PAPERBACK FROM MARINER BOOKS

60363681R00127

Made in the USA
Lexington, KY
04 February 2017